KATHLEEN HIRSCH
A HOME IN THE HEART OF A CITY

KATHLEEN HIRSCH is the author of *Songs from the Alley*, and co-editor of *Mothers*. She has been a staff writer for the *Boston Phoenix* and has taught writing at Harvard University and Brown University. Her articles and essays have appeared in *The New York Times*, *The Washington Post*, *The Christian Science Monitor*, the *Boston Globe*, *The Georgia Review*, *Five Points*, and *fiction international*. Ms. Hirsch lives in Jamaica Plain with her family.

A HOME IN THE HEART OF A CITY

A HOME IN THE HEART OF A CITY

KATHLEEN HIRSCH

NORTH POINT PRESS

A DIVISION OF FARRAR, STRAUS AND GIROUX

NEW YORK

North Point Press
A division of Farrar, Straus and Giroux
19 Union Square West, New York 10003

Copyright © 1998 by Kathleen Hirsch
All rights reserved
Distributed in Canada by Douglas & McIntyre Ltd.
Printed in the United States of America
Designed by Jonathan D. Lippincott
First published in 1998 by North Point Press
First paperback edition, 1999

Library of Congress Cataloging-in-Publication Data
Hirsch, Kathleen.
A home in the heart of a city / Kathleen Hirsch.—1st ed.
p. cm.
ISBN 0-86547-550-4 (pbk)
1. Community life—Massachusetts—Boston.   2. Neighborhood—
Massachusetts—Boston.   3. Jamaica Plain (Boston, Mass.)—Social
conditions.   4. Jamaica Plain (Boston, Mass.)—Social life and
customs.   5. Hirsch, Kathleen—Homes and haunts—Massachusetts—
Boston.   I. Title.
HN80.B7H57   1998
307.3'362'0974461—dc21   98-20414

"Making" first appeared in the summer 1998 issue of the *Georgia Review*.

Author photograph by Esther Pullman

To the memory of my brother,
Timothy James Hirsch,
who, too, once loved a place,
and
to my son, William,
that one day he may

CONTENTS

For each home ground we need new maps, living maps, stories and poems, photographs and paintings, essays and songs. We need to know where we are, so that we may dwell in our place with a full heart. —SCOTT RUSSELL SANDERS

JAMAICA PLAIN, MASSACHUSETTS

SOME 43,000 PEOPLE COME HOME to sleep every night in my neighborhood of Jamaica Plain. On the map we are a kidney-shaped barnacle affixed to Boston's famous medical area, with the Brigham, Dana Farber, Children's Hospital, and Harvard Medical School to the north. Our eastern border bleeds into our sister inner-city neighborhood of Roxbury, our west into "old money" sections of Brookline. No one who comes to Boston to view the S.S. *Constitution* makes a side trip to Jamaica Plain. Our nature is resolutely local.

And for this reason, a far more relevant orientation is that of street level. Here we discover something notable. For a good many years—an entire generation—Jamaica Plain has been composed of precisely those characteristics that demographers predict will dominate the American urban landscape by 2025.

We are young and economically and racially mixed. About 50 percent of us are white. Almost one-third of us live in households that fall below the poverty line (a figure considerably higher than the city average of 21 percent). We are one-third Latino—second-generation Puerto Ricans and more recent arrivals from Latin America, Trinidad, and the Dominican Republic—and 17 percent African-American. Nine thousand of us, give or take, are children under the age of seventeen.

That we live in harmony and a cultural abundance that is the envy of our neighbors, that we proudly experience ourselves as a vital community at a time when community seems the most elusive probability to emerge among the portents of our collective future, would seem to warrant the same scrutiny as that bestowed on the icons of our past. Or maybe I just find people more interesting than ships.

A brief sketch, in numbers:

Greenspace: 475 acres (in 5.5 square miles; 11.46 per thousand residents)

Education level: 41.5 percent college graduates

Occupations: Carpenters, plumbers, bakers, teachers, artists, doctors, drug dealers, police officers, bureaucrats, journalists, parents

Local economy: Hardwares, bodegas, clothing, used book, ice cream, and thrift shops (small-scale commercial); check cashing, real estate, restaurants (service); beer making, pretzels (light industry); small-scale agriculture

Culture and Associations:
    Symphony orchestra: 1
    Community theaters: 2

Community chorus: 1
Arts center: 1
Libraries: 3
Playgrounds: 18
Churches: 19
Video arcades: 0
Bowling lanes: 2

A *Sampling of more than forty-five clubs and associations*
Kiwanis
Jamaica Pond Association
South Street Neighbors Together
Bikes Not Bombs
Tuesday Club
Ecumenical Social Action Committee
Spontaneous Celebrations

and gathering places
Lockhorn's
Bob's Spa
Costello's
El Charro
The Midway
3M Market
Old Stag Tavern
Eddy's Market
Rizzo's Pizza
Fernandez Barber Shop
Franklin's CD
J.P. Record Shop

Café Cantata
Black Crow Caffe

and artist's studios
Two Boats Gallery
Third Eye Photo Services
57 Cornwall Street Studios
276 Amory Street Studios
3D and UP
Bad Girls Studios
More than 250 local artists participate in the Open Studios
event held each fall, displaying cards, masks, paintings,
quilts, raku pots, bead art, pouches, baskets, and handmade paper.

Housing stock: Mixed; three-quarters of our housing units are
tenant occupied
Households owning no car: 46 percent

A WORLD OF MONDAYS

ON A CERTAIN MONDAY IN SEPTEMBER, it seems that every
child in the neighborhood digs out a musty backpack, and political candidates begin appearing in the grocery stores, sounding the theme of participation.

This year is no different. The hot local race is over whether
the school board should be elected or appointed. A turf battle
over the town's soccer fields and police oversight of a rowdy
after-hours club are close seconds. But most of my neighbors
are focused on the more ancient rites of communal life, recon-
necting with those around them after the summer holidays,
reinforcing the ties that, day in and day out, give the year shape,
coherence, and meaning. They have stored their tents, closed
up summer homes, and taken rakes to their city lawns. In these
waning days of summer, they linger a little longer at the foot
of their driveways or down at the ice cream store on Centre
Street, chatting until it starts to grow cool. Then they go home,

open their black books, and reconvene yoga classes, Sunday school, and crime watches.

When I moved my hand-me-down bookshelves, twenty cases of books, and a handful of flea market vases to Jamaica Plain in the summer of 1990, I was looking for a place to belong. For ten years I'd lived in Boston's Back Bay. It had been fun and fast and anything but routine. But after a decade I'd consumed enough cappuccino, and idled away enough Sunday afternoons poking through galleries, and paid enough parking tickets to last a lifetime. My assumption that in the course of living and socializing in a place my roots would reach down into bedrock and anchor me to life in the fullest sense had proved naïve. I had plenty of friends, but no common context in which affection and principles could grow in more purposeful ways. Now in my mid-thirties, I was ready to find that thing about which, like most Americans of my generation, I knew close to nothing: community.

I looked at half-million-dollar "fixer-uppers" a stone's throw from Harvard Yard, clubby brick rowhouses in Beacon Hill. I passed through the "sexiest bathroom in Brookline." Finally, dazed and battle weary, I stumbled into Jamaica Plain.

J.P. is a snob's no-man's-land, a Boston neighborhood down at the heels for so long that only its loyalists can quite see its quirky charms, its worn-out Woolworth's and Latin botanicas and thrifts that cater to the low end: yellowing *McCall's* and tin spice racks. J.P. was by far the cheapest, riskiest, and least sexy place I ventured into. It lacked an attitude of any kind. And precisely because of this, it felt like the sort of place that might harbor that most rare and vanishing of life-forms, authentic neighborhood life.

We disappointed our realtor by choosing the smallest house she showed us: a three-bedroom on a tiny lot in the more exclusive professional section of Moss Hill. My husband and I became the proud owners of a pantry equipped with a yellow toilet, miles of red and white toile, and crimson carpet to match. On those warm summer mornings as I waited for contractors, plumbers, electricians, and painters to render it habitable, I had ample time to flesh out my fantasy of the good and rooted life.

We'd chosen to stay within the city limits because we like cities. We find them more bracing and infinitely more interesting than the suburbs, more challenging than the country. But only time would test the city's enduring potential. Could a city neighborhood become a place that I would one day call home? Could I live a whole life here—close to nature as well as humanity, with work that tangibly touched the lives of those around me, and a connected spiritual life? Would I be able to raise a child here amid sustaining relationships?

There were promising hints. A working farm operated, incredibly enough, just around the corner, selling produce to local folks. J.P. had a fair-size writers' community. And to judge from the bulletin board in the veggie restaurant, it put on a full calendar of arts events. In the park one day, I met a young mother who told me about a group of parents who were starting a cooperative pre-school in the neighborhood. I learned of a woman on my street who baked bread and actually made a living from it. Several doors down there lived an invalid whom everyone, I was told, even the kids who sold candy bars and wrapping paper for Little League, included in their projects and enthusiasms. It seemed just right—a world of Mondays with just enough flair to be conscious of itself and of how it wanted to proceed with the other days of the week.

Or at least, this was part of the picture. J.P. was a neighborhood in transition. The week we moved in, a young man was shot to death in a bad drug deal outside a bar on lower Centre Street. You could get any drug you wanted—crack, heroin, weed—in broad daylight in Hyde Square.

The mother I'd met, and the aging hippie vegetarians, had settled here in the late seventies. Self-described "urban pioneers"—artists, grad students, young professionals—they'd first rented, then bought up properties left sitting when a white working class fled court-mandated school desegregation and newly arriving Hispanics. Whole crazy quilts of streets in Jamaica Plain had been redlined; arson was a daily threat. By now, in 1990, the fires had pretty much stopped. But the residue remained, pockets of decrepitude, charred foundations, boarded-up storefronts. This, too, was part of the picture.

I'd always been a bit put off by the moniker "urban pioneer." It struck me as smug, to say nothing of dismissive of the drifts and layers of human toil on which we stood, to claim for our slender slip of history some notable act of social rectitude. But while unpacking, I came across a battered college companion to Hegel. I settled into a beach chair in my unfurnished living room, let the sun pour in across my legs, and started to read.

Hegel, it turns out, thought a good deal about America. With characteristic curmudgeonliness, he predicted that we would contribute nothing of lasting worth to human civilization until our frontiers had closed around us. Until we encountered our limits (at the time he was writing, of the geographic variety) and began at last to face one another in our cities, we would never become a civil society. And until we encountered the ensuing challenges of internal coherence—of culture, you could say—we would remain insubstantial, a puckish roué dancing across the scarred trenches of history.

When I was growing up in the fifties and sixties, the frontier was outer space. Today, no less grandiose, it is the globe: global markets, global information, global economy. The frontier—of land, goods, better land, and more goods—has not even yet, it seems, closed. Meanwhile, back on the streets of our cities, Hegel stands vindicated. For in our pursuit of ever vaster schemes of conquest, real culture, local human culture, has very nearly been lost; the problems of internal coherence abdicated, and in many places a wilderness rooted in its stead. It is the city today that has become our last and more elusive frontier.

I would soon discover what my neighbors were creating in this urban no-man's-land. I hoped first impressions were correct, that they were building a world of Mondays.

Once, Mondays were the wash days. Tuesdays were for ironing, Wednesdays cleaning, and so on, through to the Sabbath, when it all stalled for a turn in order that people might recollect themselves, bind the threads that lay tangled and frayed from all that *action*. Together, it added up to a functional, assuring social warp on which individual efforts at everything from raising children to growing tomatoes to writing poetry entwined with the strivings of others in communicable ways, ways that really did allow neighbors (to borrow John Winthrop's phrase) to delight in one another.

A world of Mondays, to my mind, invited a largeness of being that the more complicated paces of downtown life didn't. In a world of Mondays, we wouldn't be such random and self-

referential players, or self-promoters trying desperately to dis-
tinguish ourselves above the din. We would be persons, fulfill-
ing a wide array of purposes, together.

I shoveled a truckload of manure into the clay beneath the
back deck, plunked in a flat of tomatoes, cilantro, and basil,
then watered and prayed. I knocked on doors. I visited the local
branch library and the farm stand. I jogged around the neighborhood. Friends from my previous life came to visit, making
the trek out as if they were crossing Siberia, skepticism and
doubt veiled in the terms of the driving difficulties in getting
here. Other than their sporadic presence, the phone lay silent,
the doorway empty. I began to feel less a pioneer than an exile.

The fact was I knew how belonging felt, but not how it
worked. I really understood very little about the ways that held
intimate human settlements—traditional villages and bustling
city neighborhoods alike—intact and alive.

I fell back into my downtown habits. Jogging around the local
pond had been such a laudable idea. Nevertheless, mindlessly
inefficient though it was, I resumed my ritual of getting into
the car and driving a full hour, round trip, to my health club
for a thirty-minute workout. Overnight, it seemed, the cilantro
bolted, the tomatoes drew a host of aphids, and the ladybugs
I bought to take care of them vanished after the first course.

But the poetry was my Waterloo. I'd set up my office in the
spare bedroom overlooking the street. There each morning I
brought my coffee and read for half an hour, penning a few
lines before settling into the assignments that went to pay the
mortgage. I loved the hour's silence, the exchange of bird calls
I'd never heard on the ledge outside our window in the denser
human habitat downtown.

And then. It began as a trickle. One small voice at a time. A child's voice, pitched like a piccolo, penetrated my calm. Then another, and another. Babbling, chattering, full of itself: the sound so peculiarly charming and so gratingly invasive that no barrier ever invented has completely blocked it out. Of course I'd known about the elementary school tucked in a knoll at the end of my street. But I'd somehow lost track of the fact that that particular Monday in September would arrive when it would open and function for some 250 children each day.

Soon the lane was a symphony of human trills. I tried hanging a quilt over the windows. Then two blankets. I opened the Yellow Pages and called several companies listed as "internal environment" experts. The people on the other end of the line just laughed.

Had I been wrong? About this chimera, community? About myself? I had. I was sure of it.

It wasn't the decibel levels. It was the intimacy. When I'd decided that I wanted to belong somewhere, I hadn't expected to be quite so—encountered. There had been myriad ways to keep one's distance and secure one's space downtown. Not here. I could make out every word, the timbre of every timorous voice, the bravado of every anxious parent. A different norm of familiarity, apparently—no, of rawness—turned my fantasies on their head. The prospect of facing this juvenile invasion every day of the ensuing school year was too much. I picked up the phone again and booked a flight, not just out of town, but out of the country.

Partly mollified, I stepped onto the front stoop to water the geraniums. The human tide had ebbed, and as I bent to my task, I could pick out among the laggards a discordant note.

All was not happy on this first day of school for at least two
who advanced down the lane. A mother was hectoring a child
so small that I couldn't even see its head above the privet. The
child was sobbing in such pure misery that I knew nothing
could account for the stream of ire being ventured upon it.

From out of the dim and unexpected past suddenly came a
memory: my first day of kindergarten, in a neighborhood not
unlike this one. My mother had chided me into accompanying
a small boy I would have preferred to avoid altogether. I was
his sweetheart, the older children taunted, when the two of us
arrived to wait for the school bus, cruelly, anxiously projecting
their unease onto me, the newcomer. I could taste the cool air
again, smell the dry leaves, and with surprisingly little effort
conjure up the unfathomable gray hopelessness that the
thought of school presented to me on that terrible morning.
Out there, beyond the safety of home, lay nothing but treach-
ery.

I put down the watering can and walked to the foot of my
drive. There was nothing that I could say, of course. But perhaps the fact of my presence might win the child some respite
from the abuse before he or she plunged into the terrors of
the schoolyard.

The pair appeared directly in my line of sight, and the
mother, overheard, finally heard herself and fell into abashed
silence. I looked at the child and my heart stopped. A slight
and beautiful girl of no more than five fixed me with brown
eyes flooded with gratitude. My first real connection in this
place was made at last.

There are personal borders to be grappled with every moment of our being. I supposed just then that I'd come up

against one of them in the realization that in order to live in community I might need to surrender a certain degree of cherished control. Maybe what I'd expected was going to come in forms quite different than I'd imagined. Of course, I reminded myself, this is what we are continually taught about prayer. I was willing, that morning, to believe it.

I did leave the country. But I came back. And in seven years I've learned that the ways of belonging in the modern city involve living a kind of village wisdom that is older than cities, older than electoral politics and sociological trends. In the daily workings of a successful urban community, they become so deeply ingrained that we take them for granted, forgetting how uncommon they are and how hungry others are for such a life.

Community wisdom begins with being encountered. Its teachers and lessons come in unexpected, mostly humble forms, and part of growing into a place is learning how to graft its native root system onto our heretofore shiftless patterns of growth. It is a work of cultivation. My teachers have been everyday citizens absorbed in preserving the work of local culture, and they would be good citizens wherever they found themselves. This is their story, the story of what is still possible in our lives, even in the heart of a large American city.

One night before we were to leave town, we went out for Mexican food down on Centre Street. As we walked back up the street toward home, we noticed that something had been left on our front stoop. It was an offering: a loaf of bread and three tomatoes from the garden next door.

1 / CITIZENS

WALKING

_=.=.-.-.-.-.-.=_

"EVERY WALK IS A SORT OF CRUSADE," Thoreau once
wrote, an engagement with the higher purposes of our mostly
erratic human course. As he tramped his daily ten around the
environs of Concord, Thoreau came to believe that regular am-
bles in nature were one of the standards of citizenship. If men
and women could for a few moments each day step out of the
hurly-burly, if we could experience the wind, a sunset, white-
caps across an ample pond, as epiphanies of the force that holds
us all fast, we could free ourselves of the preoccupations that
yoke us to narrow aims and discover within the capacities to
create a civilization equal to the integrity and abundance of
nature itself.

Each day I set out on a walk through the neighborhood. At
the time Thoreau wrote, this was the frontier just past Boston,
a series of rolling hills and streams and stunning elevations for
all practical purposes as autonomous and rural as Concord. My
walks across the same landscape today take me down streets of

double-deckers and front stoops that crowd out the sidewalks. Occasionally, I traverse a section of well-maintained single-family homes, past gardens thick with hostas and roses, but even here nature has modulated itself to the clippers and hedges of humankind.

Annexed to Boston in 1865, J.P. quickly became part of city life. Tanneries and soap factories started to show up along the town brook where market gardens had flourished for generations. Soon a railroad line thundered in with machines and the immigrant labor to work them. The lanes just off commercial Centre Street thickened with triple-deckers. Tenements arose, and the once unsullied habitat of pheasant and grouse was soon backed up by tiers of drying laundry.

The only thing that seems not to have changed is Jamaica Pond itself. The pond is a 120-acre kettle hole situated a block away from Centre Street, symbolically, if not quite geographically, at the heart of town. Once the wealthy built their estates around its shores, and almost everyone else made it the destination for their daily perambulations. After luncheon, before tea, to clear the mind after a morning of study, to collect their thoughts before writing—these walks in nature were regarded as the ideal antidote, and stimulus, to the work of civilization.

It is here that I too repair at walk's end. Along its footpath I try to take up a dialogue begun more than one hundred years ago, about the ways we learn to be citizens of a place, and the role that our walks play in this purpose for those of us with zip codes in the concrete caverns.

On a morning in fall, the air is nippy when I arrive. But this doesn't deter the regulars. A great shawl of green, willow and oak, wraps the water in its calm just yards from a bustling parkway. Thin layers of fog pull apart above the still water. The breath of joggers clouds the air. Beneath the surface, salmon and bass drift in granite caves. Wild swans cast their long-billed shadows. Loons and cormorants and geese skim and bob in search of prey.

Jamaica Pond is one of the most beautiful places in Boston, yet few Bostonians and fewer tourists venture this far from downtown. The former have been warned off by the gang-related shootings in the projects just over the trees. As for tourists, the roads out are serpentine and subject to crazy-making detours. The taxi drivers are often unsure of the way. And to see what? A swath of green and a local watering hole?

Thus, we are secure from gawkers and strangers. They have helped to make the pond an intimate place, an oasis not for the city in general but for the neighborhood in all its particularity. Those who walk the footpath on this Tuesday in September are residents like me, not the occasional enthusiasts of July. By midday, turbaned Sikhs will sit on the benches murmuring prayers. Children will flirt with the cold shallows, chasing minnows and disrupting the Jamaicans who fish every day for their dinner. By four, old black men will be sitting on these benches clutching their canes. From every quarter of the neighborhood we come, before work, at the end of the day, and all the hours in between. We say that we come for the silence. But it isn't as simple as that.

Between the coping, embattled self we present to the world and the self we occasionally glimpse as our own lies a buffer zone for those of us who live in cities. In this zone we negotiate possibility. Our defenses do battle with our longing to be authentically engaged in the here and now of our lives. At the pond, we are able to ease the buffer, to exercise the possibilities. This was exactly what Thoreau had in mind, I think. The exercise of possibilities.

I turn north along the footpath, and in minutes the sounds of traffic have dimmed. All I hear is the lapping water and the rumors in the turning leaves. Up ahead, a pin oak juts out from shore. Its roots, exposed by erosion, are compelling, large-jointed arms on which this specimen was once lifted up out of the earth. Reaching them, I step off the path and settle in to watch the sunken pebbles drift in shifting patterns beneath the subtle waves.

At the pond there are no phones, no rush-mail service trucks in sight. No boom boxes of any kind. Almost no one wears a Walkman while strolling the footpath. There is nothing to drown out or to wall off, and plenty to hear: bird calls, human voices engaged in quiet conversation. Instead of technology, we have the company of stones and ancient green. In them we taste a sustenance deeper than any of the city's gilded lures.

These are the moments for which I come, and for which I wait—if I know enough simply to wait, becalmed, my ploys and defenses lax as the lank grass. To know that some energy courses below the surface of even the most congested human place, with its own order and rhythms, arrangements and relations. Over the months and years of daily strolls this perception argues for more: I begin to observe in such moments of clarity that certain arrangements, natural and human, allow for greater harmony and satisfaction than others. I see that there is a flow to what used to be called "right livelihood," whether among birds or bipeds. And I know that if I stay here long enough, I will come to a deeper understanding of what right livelihood is for me, and for this place I share with 42,399 other souls.

If for nothing else, we need our walks around the environs of our neighborhoods. We discover again in countless ways that we are, after all, a part of something bigger than ourselves that, if we could but learn from it, would teach us how to connect, dissolve the buffers, and be present, not just in moments at ease but all the time.

I could stay at the pond all day, and sometimes I do. But this morning I get up from the pin oak and continue my walk. A generous nature laid the blueprint here, but once you learn how to see it, the touch of a human hand is everywhere apparent. The sheltering shade of the duck banks, the new willow on the nesting island, the cleared sight lines from an old estate—all of the subtle fits and flows are the work of a citizen.

I make my slow way toward the Tudor boathouse. From a distance I see the shocking-pink geraniums that hang in a wire basket from an obscure green door. It is unlocked. I climb the staircase that holds the damp of seabed faintly. Up top, I find Christine Cooper at her desk at this early hour surrounded by maps and shells and plants in varying stages of unchecked expansion. Yet there is no sense of clutter here, in part because her whitewashed aerie is dominated by incomparable prospects of the pond and its woods. And because Christine herself occupies an atmosphere that is as clear as it is charged, and populous with projects.

On this early fall morning, it is Christmas cards. She offers a cup of coffee and leads me to the shelves that run along one wall and hold her annual scrapbooks, a small naturalist's library, and samples of birds' nests, rocks, and shells.

"Here"—she thrusts something into my hands—"what do you think of this?"

It is a crude first stab at the matter. She has glued a photo of the pond's quintessential winterscape, an ash tree sheathed in ice and wrapped in mist, to the front. I open and read:

> *This evening the snow is falling*
> *   on us trees*
> *and cold's fury is seeking out*
> *our every bough and limb*
> *we are to be nourished to breathe*
> *in the songs of ice crystals*
> *by dawn even the most tender*
> *of branches will be ice bound*
> *and for a very loud silent*
> *moment we will stand iron*
> *   clad to glory*
> *as we await*
> *the vast blue sleeve of another*
> *   evening*
> *   to move us*

It will not do to praise her poem directly: she wouldn't believe me. Christine is a poet and an artist, but she is shy about both, a modesty that stems perhaps from her working-class childhood in the projects less than a mile away. The daughter of a longshoreman, she first knew the pond as the place where she accompanied her father on his morning walks. Later she returned, a schoolgirl in braids, to play every afternoon with her friends.

"It was glorious," she tells me. "Every day, it was just running with your friends, finding your own favorite spot, and then play, play, play."

She married and left the pond behind, following her husband from army base to base at the height of the Vietnam conflict. They were eight painful years of dislocation and broken faith, intensified by counseling work she did with soldiers fresh from the front. But nothing prepared her for the shock that awaited her when she returned home.

The late sixties had not been kind. Busing, and the flight of whites to the suburbs and of skilled jobs to the South, had caused a shabby quality to take hold of Jamaica Plain. The streets were dirty. Few people were about. Centre Street was a cavern of metal grates and boarded storefronts. The rash of arsons, the litter, and particularly the abandoned homes seemed epigrammatic of the deeper social scars that had disfigured her generation. Her marriage was over. And as she walked the streets with the three-year-old daughter she'd brought home, she saw that her child would be denied the coherence and continuity that had given Christine's life shape and meaning up to then.

The pond was in many ways the most visible symbol of what had happened to the neighborhood. Overnight it had become a haggard, decrepit thicket. Residents didn't dare wander into its tangle of brush and trash. Children were warned to steer clear, the elderly kept a cautious distance. Only a few intrepid joggers and dogs ran free.

Christine took a job teaching art to special-needs pre-school children. But after work each day she took her daughter down to the pond before going back to the flat she'd rented several blocks away.

"I felt like there was no home anymore," she tries to explain to me as we watch a front of rain clouds race past her windows. "There was no home. The physical walls of holding—even that, in the end, was no home. *You* were the home. It was what you were capable of maintaining and upholding, what sense of dignity, respect. What you considered being civil. We end up being the ultimate house."

From this kernel of insight she began to wrest a life. After she put her daughter to bed, she would get out her watercolors and paint and write poems, often until three in the morning. She began to show her work and read her poetry whenever she could. Mostly this was at women's shelters and in church basements. On weekends, she took her daughter on marches and rallies in support of everything from disarmament and women's rights to racial justice. For more than a decade, this was her life.

Then in the early eighties, she stopped. Stopped doing readings. Stopped marching. She shut down. She was burned out.

"I felt: who cares? I couldn't see anybody at Harvard interested in what I, as this working-class single parent struggling against the tide, had to say."

She closed the door to her apartment and pulled out all of her old drawing portfolios and journals and the sheaves of poetry she'd amassed in ten years. She glued them up until they completely covered the walls. And at night after her daughter was asleep, she paced back and forth, looking, and reading, and asking herself, "What's wrong?"

Then one night she saw, and her life was changed forever.

"I realized that I'd been painting and sketching Jamaica Pond. I'd written about being in it. I spent most of my downtime there, and I'd been doing that since I was six years old," she said. The pond was where she needed to be.

The next day she went down carrying a pocketful of garbage bags and a rake. On hands and knees she advanced a few feet through the tangle of briar and fallen limbs. It was a beginning.

Soon, after work and on weekends, at the break of day, she found herself at the pond in her blue jeans and work boots. The days soon stretched into ten or twelve hours. The seasons advanced. In summer she cleared away old rubble and broken walls. In winter she took advantage of the lack of leaf canopy to survey blind spots and prune dangerous limbs. She fought off the stench of urine to pick at old plaster and paint in the dilapidated boathouse. There were no park rangers to assist her in cajoling vagrants from their encampments, and only occasional crews to help haul away limbs; no place to fetch water, no shelter from the cold.

"The landscape asked nothing of me but that I appreciate it," she tells me. "When you get out into the natural world and you start moving around it a little bit, you can almost physically feel yourself come back into place. You can hear a natural sound. You can relax to the point where you come on a human face and say hi."

The quiet months at the pond began to restore her sense of what was possible between human beings in a broken world.

"From the time that we open our eyes until we close them, we're all looking for the same thing—to somehow connect up with other human beings," she tells me. "It's the human contact that we need. And aside from human contact, it's the trees, it's the water, it's the ducks. It's saying yes. Almost as though society is saying, 'This is what's important, and it's not gone yet, and by God we need to invest in making sure that this stays here.' Because our times are so volatile, so barbaric, we have to be able to participate in our lives in those civilized places that get us through."

One day as she worked, Christine heard a runner's footsteps coming up behind her. She turned. It was Gerry Wright. Christine knew Gerry slightly. He was one of the few stalwarts who still trained for marathons around the pond's shaggy perimeter. Gerry ran a halfway house for inner-city teens a block away.

Christine began lamenting the park's condition. If the pond was going to become a civilized place again, the boathouse needed extensive repairs, and the park much more than she was capable of, working without pay and virtually alone. She wanted to reopen the concession and resurrect the old sailing program, and she dreamed of offering an open classroom for inner-city children. She wanted people to return to the banks and footpaths, their sense of belonging restored.

Gerry listened, and soon he began to come by regularly and offer a hand. He knew how to get things done. Where Christine lacked any kind of academic degree, he possessed three, including a doctorate in theology and another in social work. Though he was at home lobbying state commissioners in the dining rooms of the exclusive Tavern Club and the editorial offices of *The Boston Globe*, his chosen geography was at the grassroots, in the hands-on work that changed lives, subscribing to a philosophy that he called "radical responsibility."

He brought his camera, took photographs of her progress, and sent the pictures in to the local paper. He gathered teams of volunteers to help clean up on weekends. Finally he suggested that they give themselves a name: The Jamaica Pond Project.

By the summer of 1983, they felt the park was sufficiently spruced up to open its doors again. They held a small ceremony and planted a Peace Garden, and slowly the community began to return. By late spring of the following year, Christine had crafted a proposal for more extensive park restoration and collected seven hundred signatures in support of it. Thus armed, she approached the mayor, asking for city funds to help her continue what she called her "community-based volunteer maintenance project." She and the Jamaica Pond Project wanted the boathouse renovated, the footpaths repaired, and the embankments rebuilt. She, in turn, would continue to promote community involvement at the pond. Impressed, the mayor agreed.

This was fifteen years ago. Soon now, a fleet of twelve rowboats and fifteen sailboats (rentable at nominal fees) will be put up for the winter, and the inner-city teens who man the boathouse concession in summer, dispensing cold soda and pretzels and friendly information, have returned to school. Student cleanup crews still gather on weekends, though. And on the days in between, individuals appear, sometimes in pairs, to say hello to Christine or to be alone with the pond once more before it retreats into its winter silence.

The open classroom program is about to come to a close. From April through October, hundreds of classes are engaged in nature education around the pond. From pre-schoolers to overage high school students, they come, some for just an hour, others for weeks at a time. They collect water and flora samples, listen to Christine's pondside lectures, and work at the drafting tables in her second-floor office, preparing materials for those who will use the pond after them: better maps of the pond floor, water tables, and improved plant samples for display. Recreation groups have reemerged to run fishing tournaments. The historic association and local environmentalists are working to restore several sites in the parkland and to prevent damage to the pond's ecosystem from overuse.

But on any given day, at any time, programs and class field trips aren't the main event at the pond. Christine and her Jamaica Pond Project have made the pond habitable again not just for individuals or for groups but for that more amorphous thing: community.

The first time I saw the pond, it was a day much like today in the middle of the workweek. A nun strode by in her sneakers and a Baltimore Orioles cap. A pair of working-class black women race-walked past me in sloppy athletic gear, while close behind a tanned professional pushed his daughter in a jogging stroller. A cluster of elderly East Europeans sat crowded on a bench nearby, exercising their Russian on the ever changing scene. In all my years of downtown life, I hadn't encountered so racially and socially integrated a scene, or so much humanity palpably *together* in one place. Walkers tossed twigs to one another's dogs, strangers stopped to exchange a few words. Something special was happening here, in a large and fractious city place at the end of the twentieth century, that was making people make neighborhood in the ease with which they were together in nature.

Since that afternoon, I've come to the pond almost every day. And it has begun to occur to me that Thoreau really ought to have brought a companion along on his jaunts, if only in the interests of completing his disquisition. I've learned that if our encounters with possibility begin in solitude, they complete themselves, if they can be said to do any such thing, in the rituals by which we order our days, through the regular gestures we make toward the places and the people we love. These rituals are essential: they keep conditions right for the delicate transactions between the self and the world that we call community.

Each place generates its own patterns and the rituals most fitting its common life. We have only to give ourselves the chance to perceive and, having perceived, adopt them. Here, in these parts, it is our walks around the pond, more than our clubs and organizations, more than our political alliances and differences, that provide us the opportunity to feel at home together.

Though my neighbors and I seldom speak as we pass one another on the footpath, we acknowledge one another and what we share: an abiding attachment to this place. Whether we come from the projects or the Victorians on Sumner Hill, we affirm the right of every being in the landscape to a daily walk free of nuisance or interruption. In a world where we are routinely buffered from our fellow citizens by such vast and wary gulfs, this is no small thing. It draws us to one another at a level deeper than any notion of community I know. We begin to take care of one another the moment we care for our shared experience of this place.

This, I think, was what Thoreau was trying to say to an America that was coalescing into the shape and character of its cities. It is what Christine was poised to hear a century later. The struggle to create a home in the world must be engaged daily, within walking distance of where we are.

WORKING

IT IS STILL MISTY as I push open the back gate and crunch over gravel to the door of my office, carved out of the unused garage. I hear the seal give, and the cool air of night rush out. It is a fond moment, the mute exchange of familiars.

Because I do not live in an age of faith, I dispense with what would have been the customary prayer to my particular patrons. But if I have time, I rearrange a few stones on the windowsill and water the fern, tokens of this place I call home. Without fail I fiddle with the platoon of pencils ritually laid out the afternoon before when I left off work. No matter what I like to admit, I retain some feeling for the old ways of working, which take me by the hand anew each morning, gathering me back from my nighttime wanderings, to the deities and their designs for me.

I rise at five-thirty every day but Sunday to make my life function smoothly. At seven or eight, after an hour or two of writing, I break for my walk and breakfast, then return until two, occasionally four, in the afternoon, including Saturdays. In the evenings, I read.

Ever since Adam, it has been thus. To work is our necessity. Every day we reenter consciousness to turn effort into matter; as metaphysicians and as men, we craft the stuff of mind and muscle into bread and shelter. And, if we are very lucky, into meaning.

Fortunately, I am a morning person. The morning, with its deep saturated silences, its squirrels and ferny damp, is one of the great recompenses for laboring in the outland, far from office suites, in the same patch of earth where I eat and sleep and dream. I live, in fact, much like a farmer these days, and I have done so since the day that a simple raisin got away.

Writers become writers out of the allure of the peripheral. We see the oblique, and it is always more compelling than what's directly in front of us. Our glimpse of clues, our ventures into hidden places, carry us far from the main paths before we pick up the trail again; the trail that leads us, with luck, into the elusive heart of the matter.

Other professions, I suspect, begin in similarly offbeat sensibilities. The early passion of the basement chemist, the unquenchable passion of a puppeteer, the anguished attempt to cure a chronically ill sibling—all of these lead to full-formed mature identities.

But we go on to train ourselves, and then we go to work. And soon what danced around the edges, what was mystery and challenge, promise and delight, becomes profane—a set of applications. Challenge is betrayed to formula: how can we arrange life's manifold and terrible complexities within the manageable matrix of our skills? The play at the margins of our consciousness diminishes, and so do we.

To resist this dulling down of our callings requires vigilance and something else, something that I hadn't yet discovered when I first began coming out here each morning, crossing the chilly void of flimsy darkness.

For months while it was being built, after the carpenters went home I'd venture out to my garden retreat in the making. Amid the silence of chalk dust and settling tacks, I envisioned a chaste cell, a haven of solitude in which life as I had known it would be secure. I'd be just feet from the house; separate but near enough, responsive but defended.

I settled in, and quickly found that the finest feature of my cranny was the bay window I had cut when the interior drywall was put in. Life's gratuitous gems were tossing themselves up all the time, it seemed, once I was situated at ground level with the rest of the creatures who dwelled here. Occasionally a spider or two moved in. Just now as I write, a large male cardinal is chirping his sense of having secured the territory for his nesting mate. She alights by the screen, and together they inspect the wild chokecherries for ripeness. I learned to know that it was breakfast time when I heard my next-door neighbor coming out to her city compost bin in the raincoat that doubles as a bathrobe. A doctor and single mother, she gets up as early as I do to make it all work. Or when the schizophrenic old lady who shares a common back border, out early too with a bowl on her head, began to sing.

Because of this window—because, more precisely, of ground level—I began to linger more than I used to in the world past the threshold. When I set out from home, I ambled more. I found my way onto detours and dead-end roads, following signs for lemonade and yard sales.

Whole chunks of reality fell down before me that I hadn't noticed before. One humid August morning I came upon an old woman presiding over her front lawn in a worn upholstered chair like an irate Queen of Hearts. She had draped the contents of her basement all around her, nattering drawers and patchy pole lamps, and by nine-thirty she wanted it gone. I took a mildewed patchwork cover off her hands, soaked it in the tub for two days and nights, backed and edged and tied it, and laid all eighty-one square inches of it, finished, on the four-poster bed, where my savvy suburban visitors now ask: an old family piece? Pure city castoff, I reply with satisfaction. Ten dollars, plus labor.

On Centre Street I got to know most of the counter clerks by name, and how they take their coffee. In particular, I be-friended Myron during the once-a-week forays I made to the self-serve Canon copier at his shop. Myron is single and middle-aged. He has a bothersome stutter he works hard to keep under control, and a hairpiece that he's given up on. In-stead, whenever he has a spare minute, he tinkers with the invitations on display, or rearranges the business cards to show them to best advantage. Myron strokes and manages his stressed and harried customers as we pace for attention like cooped-up show dogs.

"What can I do for you today, sir," he'll jauntily ask even the most irascible purebred among us. He has a schedule of orders to keep, and the schedule is that which, above all else, is to be honored. There are no sloppy rush jobs for Myron. His standards are as pristine as his etiquette. After a half hour at Myron's, I'd head for home and the messages waiting on my answering machine, grateful for this world that I moved in with a new eye to the details.

When my son was born, I found that I needed a virtual staff —a nanny, a slew of sitters, a housecleaner, and layers of benevolent presences besides, without whom I couldn't hope to take even a step toward the door of my office. Work hours, always precious, became more so, and my solitary rambles around the neighborhood, a fond memory.

Too soon, the days were over. The things that didn't get done didn't because I just didn't know how to do it all. Wistfully, I'd arrange my pencils and the next day's work, turn off the light.

From under my new and sudden landslide of cares, I understood for the first time the vast army of professional urban parents I knew—doctors, nurses, lawyers, psychologists—who left the neighborhood each morning and returned at night exhausted, overwhelmed, longing for a simpler life that seemed beyond reach—in the city at least.

One day as my son and I started out for our afternoon walk, I spied a woman cleaning her garage on the next block. She was about my age, in sweatshirt and jeans. I pushed the stroller over and introduced myself. She leaned on her broom and said she was Veronica Serrato. I'd known that Veronica was a neighbor for some time, by reputation, and had long wanted to meet her. She was the assistant district attorney who handled abuse cases fifteen miles west of Boston in the city of Framingham. As I had written a good bit about women and violence, I was interested in her world, that place where the private horrors of hearth met the machinery of public justice.

She invited me to visit her at her office. "I love to talk about my work," she said, ducking into the house for a business card.

It wasn't until I'd left her, been down to the mailbox and back, that I had a chance to look at the card. I had to read it twice to be sure there hadn't been a misunderstanding. The address wasn't in Framingham as I'd expected, but across town, in Jamaica Plain's poor minority community of Egleston Square. I was intrigued.

The morning I arrived, Veronica greeted me in a casual skirt and sandals and with an impish smile. We were standing in the lobby of the Greater Boston Legal Services Center. Around us, Spanish was being traded between the receptionist and one or two clients who sat watching their children play at a Lego table in the corner, waiting to be called.

As Veronica proceeded to take me on a tour, she told me her story.

"I got in the gerbil tube of what happens when you do well at law school," she said as we walked through the Center's impressive law library.

I was to learn that Veronica is a master at understatement. The daughter of a Mexican-born welder, she grew up in inner-city Chicago. She made her way to Harvard and through law school at Boston University, where her brilliance earned her a clerkship with the chief justice of the state supreme court. From there, she glided into a plush office suite at the bluestocking firm of Hale and Dorr downtown, a star on the rise.

We arrive at her office. She gestures to a chair beside her desk. At Hale and Dorr she was earning eighty thousand dollars a year, working seven days a week. And she was miserable. She spent her days poring over corporate documents, with little human contact and no hope of more for years to come. She and her husband had bought the house down the street from me, but she was never around to enjoy it. In the evenings she was too tired to cook. Often, the two of them met downtown at one of the posh eateries they could now afford, then went home simply to sleep. Weekends were no different.

"Once we were in Maine, and I was working on a case and said, 'I have these plans, but if you need me, call me and I'll come back.' They did. They said, 'We need you. If you can come in tomorrow, Sunday, do.' I hated it. I felt like my life wasn't my own. I was a slave. Worse, a prostitute. Plain and simple, that's what it was."

She left the firm and began public sector work. As an assistant D.A., she argued forty-three cases over the course of three years. But the highly public nature of her work created greater needs for privacy at home. She rarely went out on walks in the neighborhood. At the end of the day, she'd dash home, grab her notes, and run off to her second job, teaching legal writing to law students. On weekends she kept to herself.

One day in the midst of all this, she discovered that she was pregnant.

"I wasn't calm, I wasn't reading, I wasn't listening to music," she says. "I was go, go, go." She only slowed down when she collapsed on the sofa at the end of long and fragmented days.

She still didn't know her neighborhood. She felt little connection to her life at all. One morning she woke up and wasn't able to get out of bed.

"I said to myself, This is insanity. I'm burned out."

Looking at Veronica surrounded by her bright woven hangings, the shelf of children's toys and stacks of composed-looking briefs, I find this hard to imagine. She is serene and funny and alert—the kind of woman that other women seek out as a trusting, commonsense friend. But I believed her.

She quit her job and decided to stay home with her infant daughter, happily unemployed for several months. She took walks in the neighborhood. She met neighbors. When the time was right, she started to skim legal periodicals for employment that might catch her eye.

"It had to be good for me to do it," she says with a smile. "This came along. It was perfect. It was in J.P. They wanted someone who was bilingual." She pauses. "I got very lucky."

She picks up a hand-carved nameplate that's been resting on the windowsill—a gift from her uncle, a woodworker, when she passed the bar.

"Right now, I'm in a good place," she says as her hands warm the wood. "In terms of balance and commitment, and why I'm doing what I'm doing."

Veronica's clients are poor Latina women and children from the community who, without pro bono legal services, would lead lives of utter misery. She defends them against abusive partners, helps represent them in divorce cases, and fights efforts by absentee fathers to lower child support payments.

She grows thoughtful, turning her nameplate over in her

hands. "It's complicated, being a minority who's a professional living in a community where there's so much poverty, but where the professional isn't poor and isn't worrying about food stamps or government bureaucracy."

Before this, she'd been able to keep the hard realities of her poor counterparts at a comfortable distance. But no more. Almost every day now she runs into clients on Centre Street, or walking their children at the zoo. She's had offers of jewelry, or child care for her daughter, they are so strapped for cash.

Each day she asks a question she never had to ask before: Is what I am doing enough? Would it be better to do more? And if so, what would that be?

"We get paid very well to work here," she tells me as she leads me back to the elevator. "But we're not doing this for the money."

I drove back to my office, deep in thought. Every day Veronica could walk to her office, down the very streets of those who seek out her skills and her familiarity with their condition. Daily, her work nourishes her understanding of her world. Once back in my office, I looked at my shelves of Virginia Woolf, Rilke, Flaubert, Annie Dillard, and I wondered: to what community was I accountable? The messages waiting on my machine were invariably from somewhere else, mostly New York. I knew my way to the train station and the shuttle better than I knew the route across town.

Like other urban professionals I knew, I worked long hours, telling myself that my fifteen-hour days locked in near-death struggles with syntax or computer were the "crunches," and

that life would just ease into a kind of suspended animation—
it would be there waiting when I came back to it. Most of my
peers lived the same way. If anything, we were vaguely smug
about it, entitled.

I socialized with peers and often took my meals with them.
As is the case for many professionals, it was my colleagues,
more than my neighbors, who validated my work.

A distinctly modern view of the self legitimates all this: the
idea of the self as a collection of parts. The economic self. The
social self. The parental self. And so on down the line. Each
has a priority ranking that corresponds more or less to the
amount of time we spend in its shoes during the average week.
As the work self expands its hegemony in this small dominion
of the ego, the other selves become co-opted into it (the social
self), or diminished, or they simply vanish—cold dry little
deaths that no one notices.

Veronica's life was about something different.

One day not long after our conversation, I took the baby
down to Myron's for my weekly copying job. As we shuffled
along, I was struck by how much work there *is* to do in a place
like mine, in any urban place in late-twentieth-century America: legitimate, even urgent work. Offering sound legal advice
is only the beginning. Teaching children, creating audiences
and artists for grassroots culture, markets for goods, interpret-
ing, cultivating, and caring for nature, and healing. It is work
that can't be done, or done well, except as part of the warp of
daily life.

It was later than usual. The bus stops were filling with workers about to head home, and the skies were gathering storm

clouds. I picked up my pace. I was on deadline for an article about women who give their children up for adoption, and I had taken the chance that Myron wouldn't have a backlog.

Myron took my pages. We chatted while I picked raisins out of the bagel I'd brought along for my son and presented them to him. Four forty-five turned into five minutes to closing, and the place was starting to fill up. I began to feel rushed, pressed to get the packet ready for FedEx by five-thirty. I stood up to remind Myron of the time, and as I did, the bagel slipped out of my hand and rolled into a dusty corner.

The baby began to wail. It was a shocking sound. I froze. At least eight people needed Myron now. And my son needed his raisins; and all of us in this crowded shop needed not to have this keening as we hurried to conclude the day's work.

Myron calmly maneuvered around the counter and came over. Through broken phrases he managed to say, "Let me take him. Go next door before they close, and get another bagel."

I stopped. This was not a rational proposal. I hardly knew Myron, really. The rest of the shop was filled with complete strangers. The truth was that I'd remained something of a passer-through in this community, alighting where it served my purposes to do so but not taking up residence in the way of my garden creatures.

Leave my child out of my sight, in the care of strangers in the middle of a city? The children on the backs of milk cartons flashed through my mind. But then, as I said, this was not a rational moment. I ran.

The rain had begun. I dashed into the shop next door—the only customer as the girl was about to shut off the lights.

Drenched and harried, I begged my cause. With pursed, disapproving lips, she indulged me.

Absurdly jubilant and abysmally terrified, I clutched my bagel and tore back through the descending darkness, plunged into the shop, and found . . . tranquillity.

Myron had turned the stroller so my son could watch the passersby while he finished the other jobs. The baby smiled and accepted half the bagel. My heart was still racing, and to calm myself, I stood beside him looking out into the rainy evening at the human tide. In all my time here, I'd never just stood still and watched the ordinary life of this place on which so much of my own life depended.

Small hardware store owners locked their doors, and the last tradesmen climbed into their trucks. The law office lights went out; so did those in the editorial offices of the local parents' paper. Mailmen, doctors, teachers, plumbers, appliance repairmen, librarians, ice cream vendors, and a handful of ministers, with the rising and setting of each sun, had chosen to anchor the best of their training and skills in the sustaining work of this place.

Behind me, Myron straightened the counter while the machine whirred, and I was grateful beyond words for his empathy and his tact. Maybe Veronica was right, and what these people were doing was the real work, the work of durable value to me, to my child, and, in the long run, to his children. Creating healthy human ecologies, like creating healthy gardens and healthy children, takes time and presence and devotion. Indeed, it dawned on me that perhaps, instead of competitive tugs on my time, all three might well be related.

Maybe the self was larger than a set of warring entities. Instead of being defended from our children, our neighbors, the places where we live—in the name of our "work"—perhaps we were meant to take them as our source and our direction.

I thought about the women in my article, birth mothers, and of the hopes with which they send their children into the world and a better life than what they feel they can provide. My two minutes of trust in Myron had brought it all home. We are, all of us, sending our loved ones out into the world every day. We close our eyes and we pray that they will be protected by care and love, by layers of benevolent presences who do what they do not for profit but for love.

How then can we fail to see what is demanded of us: that we become such presences ourselves, that we prepare the way, make the ground good and sane and worthy of one another's stabs at fulsome being.

If this is so, it presents the ultimate challenge to the modern professional. The skills of my working life up to this point— objectivity, detachment, autonomy—had served me well. But they wouldn't here. Not alone, anyway. Just as the way I fed, sang to, and touched my son was visceral, immediate, and concrete, so too is the work of a place. As I stood looking out on the rainy rush hour, it all became clear: the quality of our common life requires not just intelligence and drive but patience and forgiveness. Empathy helps, and so does the weaving of ambition into the humble needs of those among whom we share the human journey. This isn't a lesson that is given us; it is learned, if it is learned at all, by the loss of the false notion that our work is ours alone.

FedEx would have to wait. We had bagels to finish and rain to watch, and Myron to stand with for a while, chatting.

I linger more these days. My work, for now, is telling the stories of my place. I look into back yards and at the choices my neighbors make about their lives to try to make sense of this thing, community. Today I am seeing Eddy Ortega, who knows all there is to know about cocaine peddling in his part of town.

Once again, I head for Egleston Square. I pass the Legal Services Center, an empty playground, a looming Catholic church from another era. The houses around Egleston are poorer and generally less well kempt than their counterparts, the siding tending to pale pastels, yellows, and blues.

Eddy is waiting for me at the lunch counter of Mario Melendez's 3M Market. I buy him a cup of coffee, and he begins his tale by telling me about the Molotov cocktails his boys rained down on a police cruiser some years ago in a night of firebombing that dramatically upped the ante in the war between Jamaica Plain's angry young men and everyone else.

Eddy is charismatic and articulate. I like him at once. He grew up here, was raised to believe in God, love his neighbors, and work hard. Eddy did all three, but especially he did the last. By fourteen he was already looking for serious work. He had watched his father slave over steam tables at a hospital laundry, then follow this with a second job, and had drawn a quick calculation: it was never too early to get a head start.

But Egleston then was a place of little hope and few ways out. Its library had closed, the nearest public gym was miles away. Forgotten turf between two police precincts, the area was poor and preyed on by toughs from neighboring Roxbury. Just about the only things that remained besides the poor themselves were boarded-up storefronts, Pentecostal chapels, a scattering of pizzerias, and liquor stores. Eddy knew that he was doing well cooking steak and cheese and flipping pizzas for Pops at the corner of Chilcott and Washington near his home.

Outside work there was only school, a forty-five-minute bus ride to white, working-class South Boston and the high school to which he'd been assigned as part of the city's deseg plan. By eleventh grade, he'd checked out. Then he was in the Square full time, hustling to make honest money. He left the pizza shop and began working for a liquor store. He took a second job at a security service. He bounced around from place to place and back again, depending on the hours and the money. It never added up to much. Every day he passed about forty of his friends hanging out, racking up rap sheets long on truancy and petty theft, and building a drug supermarket there on the border of Jamaica Plain and Roxbury.

One day his brother-in-law asked him to invest a little of his savings in drugs.

"I'm not going to be out there selling," Eddy told him. "That's not me. I don't do that." But he turned over a little cash just the same.

In days, the brother-in-law was back, Eddy's money doubled.

"I looked at this, and I said, 'You know, this isn't bad.' This was good money."

Soon Eddy was out there on his own, bringing his drugs into the Square, doubling his money in no time.

"I made so much money. I don't even know how much money I made," he tells me. Keeping track wasn't an issue.

When he wanted a new car, he bought it—cash. When he wanted to travel—New York, Philadelphia, Mexico—he hopped a plane. Gold? No problem. Necklaces, rings, a chain for his license plate.

"I was really able to live a good life," he tells me. "And I wasn't the only one living that lifestyle, living in Boston and being a Puerto Rican. There were lots of us out there, because of the situation we were in, with no education, nothing better to do; no money, the need to have money."

Being on that thin, desperate coast on the margins of everything seemed to offer only two choices: a job like his dad's just this side of slavery, or the good life, which required detachment, becoming a virtual stranger in his own world. In the greater scheme of things, it seemed slim overhead. These were the years when he was known only as Sinbad.

Then, one night in 1990, just after the first cold snap, he was in the Square visiting his parents when he turned on the TV. A police officer had been shot at the corner of School Street; cruisers crawled across the screen just yards from where he sat watching. In less than a second, he was out the door.

A few loners were stumbling about, some drunk, some high, and from the smatterings of rage and rumor, he pieced together the story. His friend Hector had shown up that night with a stolen shotgun. For reasons no one knew, when two of the better-known plainclothes cops stopped on a routine tour, Hector had pulled the pistol-handled Mossberg 12-gauge out from under his jacket and fired.

Two police bullets brought Hector down. Some said Hector had dropped his gun and pleaded for his life, but the cops just kept pumping his body full of bullets.

Eddy stood in the middle of the dark streets and felt nothing. Hector was his age. The friends had grown up together on these streets with nothing better to do than to use their wits as best they'd known how. Hector had patched together odd bits of construction work, sold drugs, and gotten drunk, just like the rest of them. Now he was dead.

Before the riots that would follow in a matter of hours, before the police roundups and investigations, the endless media circus, and the haunting wreath of black ribbon that would sit for weeks atop a traffic light, mounted there by Hector's mother to indict them all, Eddy knew that the life he had lived up to then had just come to an end.

The shootings woke everyone up. While the city sent in cleanup crews and youth workers, Jamaica Plain professionals dusted off plans that had been on the table for years. Now money became available. In short order, one of the community development corporations proposed rebuilding the abandoned train station area there with new office and commercial space. A health center opened. The Legal Services Center moved into a vacant factory building. A Fleet Bank branch opened and offered job training for local residents.

Eddy, meanwhile, searched long and hard to find legitimate work. Would you hire a ruthless coke pusher? He finally landed a job at a young Hispanic fathers program in Boston's South End projects. But the 'hood was where he belonged, and he knew it.

At the end of 1991, the YMCA went looking for the first executive director of its new Egleston Square branch. "It was my time," Ortega tells me. "Time to come back to the neighborhood."

And this was how, at the age of twenty-two, Eddy Ortega became one of the best-known and most-respected faces in Egleston Square. In six years, under his direction, the Y has become the local mecca for neighborhood kids. It offers them a home off the streets, athletics space, a pool hall, discussion groups, and weekly barbecues, and Eddy provides what he calls informal "case management." He gives out at least forty jobs each year on the premises alone, from maintenance to peer counseling, and tries to link individual interests with schooling and other employment.

"I'm tough on these kids," he says. "The kids in this neighborhood today see themselves finishing high school and going to the next level," he tells me proudly. "These are college-bound students. This wasn't so five years ago."

Eddy himself has earned a GED diploma and is preparing to attend night school. "There's been a change of attitude," he tells me. "A change in who we are and what we want to do in life."

We in the gentler urban climes find such stories uplifting; it is always comforting to see signs of social ascension. We are less impressed by professional peers who give their lives to the parochial work of neighborhoods. And yet, without them, such tales from the burnt coasts wouldn't occur. Much of life wouldn't happen, there or anywhere else, for starters. Certainly the way wouldn't be made sane for the struggling among us to find a path out of brokenness, neglect, anger, and fear, to believe that they might change their lives.

Not every professional can reorient his or her work to the

mundane trials of the communities at their doorsteps but the doctors, public health workers, teachers, accountants, writers, and artists who do in my city neighborhood are indispensable to making it the place that it is.

The anthropologist Henry Glassie once described work in a well-functioning village thus: "Working, one learns not only one's position in the social scheme, but as well the configuration of the whole, how diverse occupations make a community, how a series of responsibilities make a life, how the interlocking unity of the hearth makes life possible."

It all connects. We are diverse beings with diverse needs. We function best in environments that are equally diverse, rich, and varied. Somehow, out of the brew of such places, residents are more alive, better nourished within, and better able to generate creative solutions and innovation in their lives and those of others.

Glassie goes on: "Here is [another] challenge: efficient subdivision need not produce compartmentalization, departmentalization, alienation, that ignorance which breeds hopelessness in the self and hostility toward the other. It can produce knowledgeable interdependence, a complexity that brings pleasure into necessary work and prods rather than stifling thought."

Every time I put my ear to the ground and carry home such a story, I learn all over again the extent to which our work isn't our own. So much of it is fragmented, interrupted, unfinished. It seems to take another set of hands to make whole what we've begun, or take up what circumstance forced us to abandon, to see our dreams in a new, more workable light. In offices and other identifiable loci of "work," we have colleagues, customers, and underlings who do this for us. In a city neighborhood, we need one another. Like all work that inheres in a place, it asks one thing of us above all else, that we show up to see the potential on our own unremarkable streets.

My day's work is done. Amid the interruptions of phone calls and computer glitches, hugs from my son and visits from repairmen, an hour's lingering took on a life of its own, and pressed me to encompass it in the form of a story. To a tradition, I am accountable. But the life here has taught me another norm of completion that threads its way in and out of this one with unexpected richness. I've come to relish the meetings on the street, the serendipitous coffee, the borrowings and gleanings of my days and what they ask of me. There is a pragmatic beauty to them that I wouldn't trade for all the contemplative solitude in the world.

Our work is never done. The aim is always completion. And it cannot be done, any work, except in real community.

MAKING

... in the long run the problem of beauty is the problem of conscience. —SOETSU YANAKGI

AT THE END OF MY WORKDAY, I push aside the stacks of notes and drafts and sit for a while looking out the window. The frame of my house has been laid for this day, literally and figuratively. I have taken the measure of the life in my immediate environs, recalibrated my place in a geography, however slightly. My work is done.

I see that the coppers and russets and sages have intensified appreciably since the cardinals first rummaged in them this morning. Soon now we will feed on a cooler palette of boughs and dry berries. I am grateful for these drapings of nature's house, color at its most beautiful, moving in its appointed paces even here in the city. It is the hour, and the inspiration, to turn to a more domestic frame of mind.

In the real places in our lives we are constantly shifting among frames of reference. Just as the public asserts itself in our living spaces, so too our domestic arrangements inform our civic enthusiasms. In this context, we are confronted with the matter of our choices in the furnishings with which we surround ourselves—our objects, and habits, and ideas.

I turn from the window and reach for a wooden hoop that lies in a basket of yarn. This is one of my responses. I stretch a piece of linen, tighten the frame, and for a few minutes find my place again in the universe of handmade things. My needle parts the linen at minute points, in and out and in again, as simply as breath itself. It is slow-moving, rhythmic, and in it I find a homeliness that I find in little else in my daily rounds. In half an hour I'll incorporate just three short lengths of floss into my design, and this painstaking progress realigns me in some subtle and most satisfying way to the original labors of my kind.

It was my grandmother who first schooled me in the work of hands. On a street of crocheters and weekend seamstresses, she was a phenomenon. Every evening she picked up her needles and yarn, set her jaw in the don't-interrupt-me-I'm-counting hold, and went to work. I remember whole seasons devoted to white cotton bandages, delicate as baby sweaters, sent off to the missionaries who worked with lepers. For variety, she turned out afghans, mittens, caps, booties, and an annual round of winter sweaters.

There were no idle hours in my grandmother's life. But handwork provided the context in which a certain "centering down" could occur. With her incredibly nimble fingers twisted with yarn, looping, transferring stitches, stabbing the next stitch at a lightning clip, my grandmother mulled the day's revelations, solved problems, released nervous energy, laughed and fell silent, nursed grudges, and dreamed.

Through the long waning years after the death of her husband and the loss of her lifelong home, yarn was her solace and enduring purpose. And through her I came to understand not just the impulse to create beauty out of deceptively humble stuff, but the fulfillment that comes from manual work, its order and exactions and its mystery, in which over time maker and work pass into each other: body, grain, and weave. It is a sacred form of work, better suited perhaps to monks than to city folk. But this only made for a more interesting conjecture. What were cities like when a good number of their inhabitants were artisans, and the terms of their work set the standards of citizenship?

Before I moved into Jamaica Plain, I used to journey to Martha's Vineyard each October and crisscross it for a week by foot and on bicycle. Along my route lay a sheep farm that rolled out along the hip of Chilmark, then tipped down toward the sea at South Beach. On the rise just above the marches roamed herds of balky, stubborn, mesmerizing sheep—lambed out, filled out, grazing with wet noses into the nippy breeze. Between the fieldstone farmhouse and the meadow's enclosure walls, I would stop and tell myself that I was ready to leave the city behind and find a patch of land on which I, too, could raise sheep and spin their wool. The haunting beauty of the slow-moving creatures against the scrim of gray-blue sky, the ancient rituals of siring and shearing and spinning that this farm sustained against the onslaught of rayon and Polartek, always struck me in a place almost deeper than emotion itself.

Back in the city, where handcrafted objects were rarities, confined to shelves for the purpose of display, and where labor, that often isolated unqualifiable endeavor, eats our days, I learned that I needed to touch that older ground regularly, to stand at the crossroad on which my grandmother stood comfortably all her life, a place where human effort was bound to human scale.

I began to stitch for a short while at the end of every day. It became a sort of private contemplative practice. I knew no one else who needed the feel of cloth or clay on their hands to right the rhythms of their days. A few friends received my modest productions. They accepted them kindly, as quaint and slightly odd. I moved into a place like glass in this work, alone and silent, calm as a person on a certain kind of journey. But —alone.

Once I was settled in Jamaica Plain and had moved furniture this way and that for a few weeks, I made it a project to frame a recently finished textile piece. An artist friend had recommended a local shop, and I set out with my map and my handwork one Saturday morning looking for Greenview Street. After several false tries, I finally located it, an alley near the post office. You would miss it entirely if you didn't come with a purpose, for nothing announces what goes on inside except a pair of black metal swans that jut out from above the lintel of a small yellow door and bear what reads more like a rumor than a trade name:

JAMESON & THOMPSON
PICTURE FRAMERS

A buzzer lets me in. I take the stairs, narrow and grayed through to nearly nothing in more places than one, and find myself in a long, unvarnished space. On first impression it looks to be a working artists' studio. Sunlight pours across white-washed walls and unfinished floors. In the corner a crimson armchair lists toward a stack of old literary magazines.

The first minute or two, I am alone. And it is good time, spent in a makeshift gallery that runs the length of the space, displaying the works of local painters, lithographers, and collagists.

There are no "service counters," no sets of obvious chromatic metal frames. Two unadorned tables occupy the middle length of the space. From these, artwork apparently passes into the hands of the framers, eventually coming to a state of finish that has to meet the standards of the man now coming toward me from the woodshop, with a half smile in which the humor and keenness are all in the eyes. Dwight Jameson, just beginning to gray at forty-five, lanky and laid back, is known by the cognoscenti as the finest craftsman framer in Boston.

I lay my piece on the table. For several minutes he studies it without a word. An assistant happens by; she stops now and looks, too. They begin to ask me questions, thoughtful questions, about technique and composition, about my vision for the work.

I am seized by a rare attack of shyness. Never has my work received such interest or intelligent receptivity. But their earnestness wins me over. The protective glass around me melts, and once I'm finished with the details of the job, I hang around. Other people from the neighborhood drop in—collectors, artists, regular folks. Some of them are dropping off projects, others picking up work, and some just come to chat. From month to month, I learn, the gallery exhibit is never the same, which is partly why people drop by empty-handed: to take in one of the vital signs of their small place in the world.

This isn't just a shop; I quickly discover it is a gathering place. And what comes and goes from its workshop aren't the isolated inspirations of anonymous, scattered makers but the stuff of a common and broadly shared local language. I've arrived in something of a niche for craftsmen. Most, I soon learn, work out of their homes, weaving and printing and making glass, but their products are sold in the craft shops and ethnic clothing boutiques along Centre Street. Homegrown herbal products and oils share shelf space with imports from outside the neighborhood. On Saturdays, sidewalk vendors appear, hawking everything from batik shirts and silver jewelry to unpainted shutters and pots. I can hardly believe my good fortune.

During a lull, Dwight lays out six eight-by-ten color photographs. Their gold light, in a Venetian morning, breaks against the green waters of the Grand Canal and scales wonderful specimens of Ruskin's legendary stones—gargoyles, cupids, fantastical masks—transfixing them and me in its other-earthly haze. From the back room Dwight summons an apprentice named Tom, a polished twenty-something in exile from banking. Together they bend over the pieces, and we hear Dwight's voice, quietly, patiently, explaining that in here it all begins not with breathless admiration but with—a ruler.

With precision, quality, respect. The proper proportion of mat to image and then to frame, the width and lift of the risers (those invisible wedges that create a sense of float between image and frame), the accuracy of the measurements that travel with the piece through its various stages of completion—all are essential to a well-wrought frame, and no piece leaves here without them.

Dwight pauses, squints, and holds one of the photographs up to the light.

"Is that a water spot?"

Tom leans in.

"Better tell her. I hadn't seen that."

Tom makes a note. They bend down again. Dwight places the ruler again. Not a sound can be heard, except now and then the distant brakes of delivery trucks.

Finally he straightens. "Looks like we're going to go up five-eighths on the bottom," he says. Tom nods, takes the ruler, and commences his task. This morning, and for as many mornings as he can imagine, Tom will measure. He will lay a fine-calibered ruler up to the margins of images, over and over and over again, his work scrutinized by Dwight, until he has mastered the discipline of detachment, consistency, and attention. Only when these have become second nature will he move on to another stage in becoming a Jameson & Thompson framer.

"People have to be here for a while before they're worth anything," Dwight tells me as he walks back toward the wood-shop.

Everything has been in motion for some time this morning, mat cutting, glazing, beveling, and finishing. People move up and down stairs consulting the schedule board or carrying frames from one room to another with a relaxed air of order as the sun pours in through the towering windows and classical music plays on the radio.

Nearly everyone who works here is an artist in his own right,

Dwight tells me. Mostly, they are painters who live in J.P. In the fitting room, Brad has just finished applying silver bezels to a pair of mats that will frame two watercolors. Now his hands glide effortlessly, slicing strips of oatmeal-colored fabric. He glues them onto impossibly thin blades of walnut without a smudge of misplaced glue, then irons them to meticulous edges for an archival piece he will finish in the afternoon. Brad has worked here for six years and learned most of what he knows about his painstaking specialty work from Dwight himself.

Before this, he supported himself by working in various retail jobs. He shudders, remembering. "It was so claustrophobic," he says. "It's an awful, awful, awful way to make money."

A Puerto Rican painter who calls himself simply Z listens as Brad talks. He pulls a cutter down through a series of mats and moves them to the glazing table. Dwight's salaries are slightly higher than the norm in frame shops, he says, but no one is here for the money. Rather, says Z, "They're here because of the vision Dwight has."

Dwight Jameson started out as a social worker, determined to change the system for kids who were packed off to jail or detention homes for offenses you could spit at. He struggled tirelessly to keep them out of trouble and the grip of the state. But nothing seemed to change. It wasn't the kids; it was a system that never came through—not with resources, or follow-up, or support.

His father had been a printer who'd spent his entire working life in one shop, lining up copy, pulling proofs, and inspecting them for flaws with the magnifying glass he kept on a rope around his neck, even at home. To Dwight growing up, the monocle was the emblem of what he called his dad's "craziness."

When Dwight went off to college, he left that world behind. Instead of toiling in a lowly trade as his father had done, to no particular financial profit all his life, Dwight clung to his dream of changing the world by helping people to use their own minds. But after five years in the quagmire of case meetings, reports, and paperwork, in the company of long-tenured bureaucrats and imprecise aims and lax standards, he wondered what he was about. He had more power than a human being ought to have over the fate of another, yet he felt hog-tied by the system, impotent. He was failing the kids. He had failed himself.

He quit and left his hometown, never to return. Floundering, he followed a girlfriend to Boston and rented an apartment in Jamaica Plain. Here he fell in with the art students who occupied the triple-deckers in the neighborhood east of Centre. J.P.'s down-at-the-heels bohemianism and after-hours jazz clubs appealed to him. A night didn't go by without a party or some sort of music/literary/art "happening." But these circumstances didn't change the basic fact of his life. He was untethered. He took a succession of jobs, then left them, took up art classes, and left them.

Then one day Dwight found himself in the cellar of a small shop on Beacon Hill. He watched as an old Italian named Tony cut mats. This latest job, once he learned how to do it, would be to cut those same mats and with the same precision, leaving Tony free to do the framing. Nothing had been too serious in his life for some time, and he'd taken this job at the Ainesworth

Gallery with the same supposition with which he'd taken the four or five previous ones: he'd pick up a few pointers and move on.

But watching Tony as he mitered difficult scrollwork and sanded corners with complete absorption in his task, Dwight felt something different. Tony had been doing the same thing in that cellar, day in and day out, for eighteen years. There was a purity in his devotion to discipline, his pride in even the smallest job. Watching Tony, Dwight finally understood his father. For the older Jameson, honor and fealty to a tradition and consistent mastery in the face of humble daily tasks were the just deserts of a craft well done, dearer than all the freedoms that white-collar work extolled. Here, at last, Dwight felt, was work that permitted a true aim at excellence.

Dwight stayed with Tony for two years, learning everything he could from the old man. Then he moved to the Old Cambridge Framing Company. Where Tony had taught him about skill, Old Cambridge taught him about community. His colleagues in the East Boston loft were generous with their knowledge. They shared their expertise in wooden frames, special matting effects, and archival techniques, and they supported one another in an atmosphere of respect and community. Dwight found himself thinking that if he ever ran a shop of his own, it would be much like Old Cambridge.

In the winter of 1985, he moved into the factory space on Greenview Avenue, a decrepit ruin, with a box of garbage bags and a thermos of hot coffee. He had no materials, no tools, no money. Penniless after putting up the first and last month's rent, he simply started in, scraping, sweeping and gathering up trash, working past midnight night after night well into January.

He opened in March without even the scratch for another month's rent.

But orders started coming in. Old clients came searching; artist friends spread the word. And he has never looked back.

At the worktable, Dwight and Tom are now bent over two contemporary textile pieces. The customer has just left, a mass of mat samples have been pushed aside, and Dwight is absorbed in just looking at the art itself, giving the image his eye and intuition, the instincts of twenty years rolled into one unified act of "seeing" the fit, the relation between color and balance, the whole. This is the framer's creativity.

Behind him is the woodworking shop. There, he says, his philosophy is articulated most concretely, in the signature ash and cherry box frames crafted from raw timber. I step inside. A dry forest smell permeates the room from a large bay of uncut planks in the corner. A woman named Donna miters raw lengths in silence. From time to time she looks up to rest her eyes on Peter, not intently but more in the way of a benchmark in her day's repetitive task. He is bent close over his frame, sanding, making almost imperceptible passes, and he will be thus bent until lunchtime.

Nothing is taken lightly here. Making a single frame can take a week and engage the hands of as many as five people. From cutting the splines to sanding and burnishing the frames, it is a laborious, exacting process, a matter of endless refinements, until the piece is carefully set on the long table by the door to be oiled, stained, and rubbed to the point that it achieves the sheen of fine satin.

Looking at Dwight's frames, I'm reminded of Archibald MacLeish's "Ars Poetica": "A poem should not mean / But be." They are simple and unadorned, wood caught in a pure geometry of restraint. They have a way of supporting the work of art, of holding it, while at the same time allowing it to occupy its own space without competition or artifice, cheap stylistic borrowings, or decorative cliché.

Dwight himself, as he moves about the shop, tracking work slips, talking to a customer, attending to Tom, the phone, and the adding machine, seems an amalgam of these traits: inward but frank, understated but straightforward.

"My work is very much about design," he says simply. "I try to figure out first what the customer is looking at. Then I tell them what I think the piece needs. Ultimately, the question has to do with the art itself: how will it best be presented? That is my work."

One senses an order here, a "rule" as integral to this shop as the chores on my lovely sheep farm. The laid-back atmosphere has an obvious appeal, and the continual art scene patois connects the staff to the work of peers. But the order I sense derives from more than this. In the end, a good part of why people are here, and why folks from the neighborhood are continually dropping in, lies in the quality of work being done here, the pursuit of excellence that still observes the standard of the human hand.

"Dwight has intentionally tried to build a sense of community here, and he's succeeded," Brad tells me. "We argue a lot. Artists can be really contentious people, but this is a very nice group of people to argue with."

To spend his days working with integrity was what brought

Dwight into this world and is what keeps him in it. From the first time he watched Tony, he understood that to work with one's hands is a state of mind, and that the stratum of the culture from which it comes is the bedrock. It endures in what is shared, practiced, diffused; its rules are the codas of our collective memory. And it needs two things to survive: teachers and a community.

Dwight employs artists, and he displays their works, talks about them to customers, and gives them pep talks after disappointing shows. His annual spring bash, I learn from Mary, is famous for miles around. One night each May, the woodshop is turned into a stage for a live band, the worktables are laden with food, and local artists and patrons dance until dawn. And on the days in the studio when things aren't going well, his frame shop serves as a sort of drop-in center for the inspirationally dispossessed.

Once, Dwight found a home among the artists in the community. His influence, in turn, has been profound. Since 1985, when he opened, numerous other artisans—stained-glass workers, weavers, furniture restorers, potters, and handset printers —have set down roots here. Together they support a level of artistic enterprise that is rare in a city neighborhood.

Once found, it is hard to imagine living without the company of artisans. Their quilts, pots, frames, fine woodwork—simple forms composed of common materials—are not, to be sure, the only forms that culture takes. But—what we have not understood until it may almost be too late—they may well be the indispensable ones.

Once, we were all people of the hand; and our cities, as Whitman wrote, "concrete, original, sincere, unpolished." We were weekend poets and tenors and quilt makers who recognized that unlike the treadle, the jenny, or even the chisel, the hands are the most brilliant tool ever created. On the strength of this understanding, our predecessors were able to frame a question we sometimes seem to have forgotten: if each tool fulfills a specific necessity, what is man, and what necessity do we, or might we, fulfill?

Given the economic realities of modern city life, it isn't easy to live in the light of this question. Many of the old shops elsewhere have folded or compromised with cheap high-volume work in order to compete in a market of fast-food frame shops. For fifteen years Dwight has bucked the trends. Though he works eighty hours a week, he has never owned his own home. Offers have come and gone from would-be backers, investors who would introduce simple turnkey work. Each time he has chosen excellence over his own creature comfort.

Not for nothing have the ages preserved these lines from Ecclesiastes:

> Without these cannot a city be inhabited . . .
> They shall not be sought for in public counsel, nor
> sit high in the congregation . . .
> But they will maintain the state of the world, and
> [all] their desire is in the work of their craft.

As I leave, I wonder what it would be like if we all lived in such relation to our labors, in a world where even a limited number of the mundane objects we use every day possessed—

because of their beauty, because of the fact that they were made by us or someone we know—a meaning that transcended function.

I now count among my friends a core of quiet artisans—knitters, weavers, rug makers—who believe as I do that as the sun goes down, the work of our hands becomes one of the few ways in which we can meet the challenge of an urban cultural identity. When I am working with my fibers, I know to demand more: real bread, real relationships, real ideas.

I am learning a new stitch, the Burden. The Burden is composed of a short vertical weft that my needle weaves over a horizontal warp in two shades of gold. In the last wash of daylight, it resembles a basket, one gold resonant of wheat, the other of a medieval reliquary. It is a laborious stitch, and as I work it, I consider the etymology of its name. The dictionary gives two meanings for *burden*. A burden is something that is carried, like the basket my work resembles. But it is also a recurring idea, a theme, such as the leitmotif in a piece of music.

What if we were to pick up the burden of culture once more—not merely to pluck at its contents, inveterate consumers that we are, but to carry it some distance down the road as practitioners and teachers, as communities of hands? What if we could learn again through the work of hands the essential validity of measured, incremental acts? This was the moral context in which the earliest objects were formed. Before there were machines, or mass marketing, or virtual communication, the work of community—of creativity, conflict, and healing—was the work of hands.

PLAYING

IT IS FRIDAY NIGHT AT DOYLE'S, and my date is a two-year-old with a fondness for scrod and the usual menaces of mischief and willpower. We enter a dimness of kelly green and deep-stained leather booths. At one of the longest mahogany bars this side of Galway, the barkeep polishes the draft handles and stays clear of the half-dozen regulars who hunch over plates of stew and nurse beers. Here in the front room, the air is as thick as the glass bricks that block out lower Washington Street; the decor, old war bond posters and bottles of French's and Heinz.

Lunchtime entertainment at Doyle's is Oldies 107, but this is a concept that comes and goes, and the quiet is as good as it gets at this end of Washington by the bus yards. Now, at 6 p.m., the supper crowd has brought on the venerable tube that hangs by the air conditioner at the business end of the bar. We watch a blocked pass and a handoff as we wait for a table, my companion joining in with the barside quarterbacks

("Go long!" he cries to the punter), when at last we're shown into the back room, where the light is brighter, the air clearer, and the sounds of congregate youth and vulnerable china identify its temporary emanation as a holding pen for families.

Why, you might well ask, do I consider a tavern a suitable form of recreation for a toddler? For starters, the food is home cooked and the beer is great. Tonight the menu is broiled scrod, corn chowder, and Grape-Nut custard. Doyle's is one of the few places within a fifty-mile radius where the hostesses bus and the waitresses call after you, "See ya later, guys!" and where fresh coffee is brewed for the friend who needs a few days' grace from the Guinness, slouched low in one of the dimmer booths. Here, as at few other places in town—or anywhere else, for that matter—we are at home away from home: one family, one tribe, one community.

In the family room the kids are keeping themselves entertained with an old station light up on the wall. It flashes green-red-green-red while their milk is being wiped off the floor. Even the nonsmoking policy wonks from city hall, who by some misfortune find themselves seated in our midst, their mechanical pencils imperiled by the occasional airborne fry, don't mind the revels of a flushed soccer team out with the coaches for a victory burger.

At this moment my friends elsewhere in town are striding into twelve-screen movie theaters or four-star restaurants. I'm at a kind of Friday night social, bunkered down with bureaucrats and retired electricians and beret-bearing old activists, like the defeated mayoral candidate of 1980 across the room under the poster of Cardinal Cushing, still making his mark, out of the pollsters' limelight.

Endless platters of fish and chips and onion rings go by. But food isn't what Doyle's is about. It's about sociability, neighborliness, the stretches and strokes of public recreation. My friend arrives with her eighteen-month-old, breathless. She plunks him into a booster seat and orders a beer.

"Isn't this place great?" She leans back against the booth and closes her eyes. The weekend has begun.

Twenty-five years ago, every face in here would have been white. Tonight we are white and black and brown and somewhere in between. But other than this, not much has changed. When we take a table, we scan those in our vicinity as a matter of course: there's no telling what chance encounter may call for extra chairs.

When Gerry, Eddie, and Bill Burke bought this place from Frank Doyle and his nephew in 1971—quite recently by the standards of place—Jamaica Plain was for all intents and purposes disintegrating as a traditional neighborhood. The old regulars who came in promptly at 12:10 from the plants in the neighborhood were being laid off, the sons and grandsons of the old horse-and-wagon team drivers were moving away, the teachers and small-time accountants were fleeing busing and the massively disruptive highway construction project that had pitched the neighborhood into a headlong decline. The Hibernian Orders and the softball teams were falling by the wayside for want of members. And newcomers—Cubans and Puerto Ricans drawn to the cheap housing—were taking their place.

The Burkes had cut their baby teeth in the neighborhood. They'd played their first stickball in its streets. Their father had sold peanuts and hot dogs at the Franklin Park Zoo in the days when Sundays were for spending in the park and pony rides could draw a small crowd. There wasn't a group in town that didn't have its own baseball team, even the Jamaica Plain Grocery Clerks; the Violet Club, the Alpines, and the Flickamaroos were in the prime of their tea-dance years. Back then, the annual rowing and sailing regatta at the pond regularly drew two thousand spectators, and for little more excuse than their own civic virtue, citizens would dress in full military regalia and parade down Centre Street behind floats and marching bands, stopping at the clubs along the way to hobnob with their compatriots in the grand romance of public theater.

Maybe the genius of the Burke brothers was realizing that what mattered more than anything in 1971, in the midst of cataclysmic change, was simply providing the neighborhood with a space and a welcome in which the gathering instincts of community might arise from the sawdust and assume new life. Once you stepped in the door at Doyle's, you were back in the neighborhood. Wherever and whatever you had been in the intervening hours—bureaucrat or bus driver, Black Panther or manicurist—here you were one of the regulars. From the anonymity of the big city streets and baggy, at best approximate, public roles, you could come home to the particular.

And so it remains. Into the common ground that we sow week after week by these motes of conviviality, life in its various dimensions here is brokered, embroidered, endured. Friends lose jobs or help one another's kids find them, go bankrupt, fall ill, sell one another insurance, represent each other's kids in court, put one another up for clubs, coach and referee their offspring, and with grateful relief attend their graduations from high school. And come Friday night, we stop by one another's tables or share a word at the bar on the way in, staying together in the ways that matter, carrying one another across the less clement shoals of life's wide waters.

Doyle's enlarges our private circles, circles overlap, webs and mandalas of association send ripples in their wake. Our gathering has engendered Boy Scout troops and a new school gym; it is the fuel that runs the church drives and the symphony appeals, the garden and historic revival plans—all hatched and furthered by people who exchange beers on a Friday night, then step out into the cold to give one another a lift home through the chill night air.

My friend teaches in an alternative high school program for at-risk students. Her husband builds slurry walls for a living. They're looking ahead to their own son's school years, and my friend has a plan. "What about our doing our own cooperative kindergarten," she asks between mouthfuls of Irish stew.

One of the great strengths of city life is the fertile interchange between the "high" play of institutional culture and the more intimate play of the neighborhoods, with all their shifting shapes and sounds, sights and rhythms, music, beat, and spice, as they express the singular qualities of each particular community's passage through them. Between the museums and theaters and universities and libraries, on the one hand, and the neighborhoods, on the other, how can the cultural life in the city fail to thrive?

And yet, too many a neighborhood has succumbed to mass-market chic—whether of the Wal-Mart or the Starbuck's variety, it hardly matters, for neither has anything to do with the singular or the local whatsoever. A certain aridity, as a result, has set in in many urban neighborhoods, where genuine interaction, even if it arises, has little to anchor it. Those who would share a café table or a bit of the bar retreat behind closed doors, into selective intercourse and defensive privacy.

A lot of thought, time, and money have gone into offsetting these modern city problems. We've built public spaces and atria, equipped them with benches and kiosks, and studied endlessly the ways people come and go and use or reject such venues of interaction. But we have perhaps not understood well enough the essential role of play in restoring the genius of neighborhoods.

Play in all of its guises—games, rituals, public parades, and contests—dredges us out of our stultifying regimens and sets our ordinary appetites of greed and power, our caution and doubt, on their heads. Almost in spite of ourselves life's more qualitative norms dance to the fore. We enter one of time's larger ballrooms, less mindful of those niggling increments, the minutes, and discover there what is finest in us—our inventiveness, our pleasure in physical expression, and our capacity for delight, even in this age of obsessive calculation.

Indigenous, authentic neighborhood play is essential to high culture. We need only think of the jazz clubs of the small-town

South, the Impressionists in Honfleur, off-off-Broadway theater, the *contradas* of Siena to see that there is a direct
connection between low and high culture, if not always in the
consumption, then certainly in the creation of it.

And the more places we have close to home where we can
furnish ourselves with the flash of original life, the better. The
Burkes knew that real play is participatory, and that one of the
best ways to get something going is to offer cheap pizza and
make people comfortable over a few burgers and beers.

Not long ago I met an old colleague here for lunch. A columnist
now, he is one of the éminences grises of the journalism of
small places. As he came through the door, conversation at the
bar stopped. Hands went out. My friend has spent many an
hour here, listening to the stories of barflies and bureaucrats,
union guys and hacks from city hall who make the journey out
at midday. And from average citizens at the bar, like my friend's
husband.

Journalists love this place. So do mayors, past and present, who sit down to the corned beef Reubens. Editors and
officials in business suits share the acrid dusk with longhairs in
hoop earrings as easily as their London Fogs perch on pegs
alongside Jerry's Auto Shop jackets. They come not because
Doyle's is the only Irish pub in town but because of what they
hear.

For out of a community's play comes not just a certain tone
but a political confidence. Play fosters a politic that is concrete
and literal, and that doesn't exist in places where the connections between people are more abstract and one-dimensional.

There's the guy who's been actively working to fix the potholes on Myrtle Street. Here's the one opposed to the zoning variance for a group home on pondside. There's the driver of the number 38 bus.

It spawns a homegrown leadership that is a powerful corrective to our otherwise shrink-wrapped notion of what a leader should look like. Those who are willing and able to devote the time and energy necessary to bring people together, nurture projects, and see them through thrive in a place like this. They're old Boy Scouts, at-home moms, unemployed disk jockeys—local doers who've been around long enough to know everyone and to sustain the network of relations on which nothing short of a community's life rests.

The result is an uncommon degree of political health. Where "politics" is accessible, it tends to be responsive. And Jamaica Plainers, seeing the small local ways in which they can make a difference, are uncommonly willing to run for an elected neighborhood council seat or a spot on the school council, or to beard the state rep when he stops in.

This is one of the answers to why I bring my son into a smoky barroom after dark. I could be living somewhere else, dining in a mall and dropping into a movie. But I'm not, and part of the reason is because of places like Doyle's, which keeps the nature of our urban identity honest. Doyle's enables us to capitalize on our condition, to celebrate and even to ritualize it, however informally.

Have I said that Doyle's isn't beautiful? That it lists on the outskirts of town, rather than along trendy Centre Street? That it's cheap? Doyle's offers no affectations and makes no apologies. It welcomes all who come through its doors. And in all, it is one of the most genuinely democratic institutions that we possess.

The bulletin boards outside the bathrooms perhaps best tell the story. They are littered with local business cards, flyers, and announcements. Of course, there is soccer. There is also basketball, ice skating, yoga, and the town pool. But a phenomenal array of poetry readings, impromptu theater groups, book groups, and seasonal celebrations have been spawned in the years since the Burkes opened their doors.

Together they create the distinctive stew of culture that sets us apart, eccentrics in the urban monoculture. It is culture that is to be found not in the formal institutions around town but in its lofts, private homes, church halls, and taverns.

As I tussle my toddler into his red fireman's boots, I skim the alternative to bruised shins: youth soccer. This year, again, Marina is coordinating. Other than being thus engaged, I see that I could be attending a performance of *The Crucible*, a gay couples dance, or a Tropical Fiesta, complete with a local mariachi band and folk dancers. A Guinean drum concert is coming up; so is a comedy bang and a poetry slam.

But the other point that ought to be made is that it is okay that I'm not. A community with a healthy sense of play offers options for all ages and conditions—and this, too, is very much a function of the quality of our interactions, consistency, and commitment over time.

I routinely regret not being at a point in my life where I can attend the Jamaica Hills Association annual dance, or its myriad ice skating parties, fairs, and picnics, the announcements of which dot the telephone poles around my neighborhood. But they keep coming, and it is good to know that they are there and that others are keeping them going for the day when I can lend a hand. It is good to know that I live in a place where our enthusiasms are shared in play that binds us, players and neighbors, around thousands of seemingly insignificant gestures that fatten the rest of the year. Doyle's, even in the family room where someone's child has just tossed a red sock into my plate, keeps me in the flow.

"So what do you think," my friend wants to know about her kindergarten scheme, but only in a Friday night sort of way. She gathers up the leftovers to have for lunch tomorrow and pops them in the baby's stroller. We're well fed and sleepy. Before we know it, Monday will roll around with its lists and obligations. The question will keep for a week.

The Greeks likened the planet to a gymnasium arranged by the gods for the exercise of men. All experiences were to be viewed as stretches, movements, turns—contests for the gods' greatest gift of all, the gift of wisdom. In man's play he was to become sage; to fail at play was to fail at life itself.

That most public of peoples knew better than we do that the only people who play happily alone are children before the age of reason. In fact, their word for *idiot* suggests an equation between stupidity and privacy.

"Idiots," writes Ray Oldenberg in *The Great Good Place*, "were those who only understood their private worlds and failed to comprehend their connection to the encompassing social order." If we need further proof than is everywhere around us today, excessively private lives lead to a sort of cultural stupor. It is good to come to a place where, even if we don't set to planning something as grand as a Broadway hit, my son and I learn again what it is to be alive.

REMEMBERING

SATURDAY'S COME ROUND, and the tables are sitting up on the blacktop like old courtesans at tea, draped in scarves and dubious silver, solicitous of the shade of off-hours and venerable town halls. Around them retainers cluck and fuss. They mutter prices and cautions to the first, familiar bargain hunters, out early to sample the week's wares.

Wares? More like revelations, these floating continents of memory. Life here flows from betrayal to discovery at hands that have sorted through old cups and found the cracked ones wanting, who yield up Grandmother's hat pins for a song. The early birds poke and glean, shifting through brooches and old buttons in the silt of a city's age.

Antiquity of no particular pedigree is scattered up and down the main streets of Jamaica Plain, and no one yet would dream of deposing it to the secondary ways. Thrift shops dot every block, and it is no small measure of the pleasure of belonging here that one can ramble into half a dozen of them in as many blocks because the rents are still low enough for their essential repositories.

Some are spruce, some sprawling; all are old and eccentric as kin. Jamaica Plain's old buttons are the worn overcoats and yellowing lamp shades, paste buttons and rhinestone clasps of those who passed through before us, the clerks who were closet bookworms, the bus drivers with a soft spot for Caruso.

Each shop commands its own muse and following. The Pauper Bostonian boasts tarot readings, Reminiscences, Victorian plate and old gilt. But for all the prideful differences in degree and kind, station and specialty, all share the humbling democracy of the past in search of yet another life. And because of this, they are vital places, sanctuaries not of lives, precisely, nor of trophies; not dispossessed but not yet claimed. They are way stations of stories and possibility.

Come Saturday, when the flea market in the parking lot at town hall adds to the theatrics, J.P.'s memories have a way with them that they don't have any other day of the week. The flimsy shop doors are wedged open, red banners hung out, and lawn chairs set under the tree at the old Baptist church for folks to rest their joints and enjoy the passing show. It is as if they find their voices again, and in response, old-timers in straw hats, bag ladies, and chic lesbians in nose rings find to their common surprise that they are touched and subtly changed.

On the ground not far from where I stand lists a doll's rocking chair. Its white paint is badly chipped across its infirm frame. The weekend project of some amateur, uncle, or father, I imagine, toiling with inadequate tools and means—flimsy dowels and tacks—for the prize of a child's smile.

I don't need a doll's rocker. In fact, I own not a single doll. But the terms of discourse, if you will, between myself and this winsome thing that seems to have just spoken to me are quite other than those of commercial convention. I don't pause to think what I need or don't; some other order of relationship is at work here, whose first principle seems to be seduction, and whose second is adaptation.

Without a touch of restoration, I can see that the rocker would be fine upon my mantle, flanked by a pear or a pine cone, a framed image of a girl. Then again (the inevitable thought occurs), it would delight a niece not yet in braces and piano lessons, passed with a certain respect for its original mission in life. Yet again, painted, it could hold a pot of pansies in the guest room.

All is possible; our encounter has just begun. Above my head, an older black woman is haggling over five ruby-colored juice glasses. She's been circling for some time. I've watched her finger the partial set, put them down, and wander off to calculate her best offer weighed against the intensity of her desire.

Thus the old things turn us into suitors. We tell ourselves to be reasonable. But the Pygmalion effect has been unleashed and will not be contained. What can I make, do, with these old forgotten things? Then too: this serendipitous moment may be revealing a piece of our own design, as if by some alignment of the stars we've been touched, chosen, by them.

To step outside the milling scene for a moment, to stand on the curb and watch, it is obvious that what a community does with its material past can only in the most benighted of senses be called commercial. These are archetypal events, abuzz with the wholly different energy of ritual and transformation. The gaiety of the bacchanal touches young and old alike: the sense that the Romans dubbed *dum vivimus vivamus*; everything will change with time, even we, eating lemon ices on a sunny morning just before lunchtime.

My black neighbor pays for her glasses and scurries off, elated. That thrifts serve an essential purpose in enabling the poor among us to live with some degree of self-respect should never obscure their deeper import. Old things—objects, buildings, ideas—embolden us to live with more than sufficiency. They have a way of fortifying us, adding their vitality to our own, and with them, the stories of the place that in time became ours.

The glasses, of course, have a history. They might have belonged to her mother. More likely, the wife of a tradesman with one or two too many children, the youngest of whom in a harried dinner hour was responsible for the lost member of the set. Or they went back to the cupboard of an aunt or cousin who'd purchased them new from the glassmakers of Bedford, on the Rhode Island border. In which case, who can say what became of the perfect half dozen?

These remnants of age and innumerable private wars hold their intimacies like fingerprints pressed on the curves and diamond junctures, as common as dirt and as mute. Holding the glass or the rocking chair in our hands, we glance as in a looking glass back through the daily lives of people much like ourselves, from the electrician's wife to the piano teacher, and so on, until we arrive at some imagined version of the life in which our object played a part. We grope toward a broader acquaintance with the cupboard, the hours, the atmosphere in which the daily serving of juice took place. If indeed it did at all.

But it is impossible; not to be done. The object has ceased to speak. We look up, a little disoriented, into the morning as it bends toward noon, full of a sense of the past hovering in the air and the old buildings around us, with a longing to make its kinship more acute. More than their invitation to whimsy, it is the soft gravity of the old objects and their stories that gather us—poor, rich, learned, dull, new, and old—to common ground.

None of this desire is lost on Michael Reiskind. Punctually at 11 a.m., Reiskind positions himself beneath the massive beech on the lawn of the 1762 Loring-Greenough House, just over the fence from the flea market. A portable microphone sits at his feet.

Lighting technician and town historian, Reiskind gives over Saturday mornings to the propagation of the past. Current president of the town's historical society, he stalks the city archives and pores over old photographs, deed maps, and real estate records. He spends much of his spare time following cues that can fill in the lacunas in the local story. He commits these to his immensely prodigious memory and to the already burgeoning (and it must be said, somewhat unkempt) files of the Society's archives at the Sedgewick Branch Library, where the patient Alice Roberts is always happy to let a curious dabbler rummage around. The Society began in 1992 with a founding board of five, including the local newspaper editor and an octogenarian. They meet monthly, and in between times gather what comes their way—old letters, clippings, the attic boxes of deposed estates—with a keen and tender avidity.

Now some dozen of us gather to begin Reiskind's hour-long walking tour. We are, as the town is, a motley of young and old, bearded and well coiffed, ardent and casual. Several of us have drifted over from the tables next door, smitten by some artifact and eager for the broader view.

The tour is confined to the area immediately surrounding our Civil War Monument, on its own small traffic island just opposite, and the cluster of historic buildings that include the town hall, First Church, and the original seventeenth-century milestone. This is as close as we come to a town "center," and if the owner of the ruby glasses didn't herself dwell here, she doubtless knew it well.

A city has two distinct kinds of history that set it apart from other sorts of places. The first is the random and the incidental, of which cities have a far greater proportion than villages or farms. The birthplace of so-and-so, for example; the temporary apartment of X, who passed through en route to Y. This history is delightful in its own way, and localities make much of these accidents in their pride of place. Here, for instance, is the home of Peter Parley, the first publisher of Hawthorne. And not far from where we stand is the Footlight Club, the oldest amateur theater in America, which still functions today. Here, the home of Sylvia Plath's father.

But there is the far more significant history of the intentional, those principled moments "of intensity when common action is exaggerated into visibility," as one historian put it. It is for this that I am eager and ready to submit to Reiskind's authority, for the distinctive moments and voices that make us the place that we are and not someplace else. These are the grand old buttons of a community's life, and as we stand listening to him describe the cornice of the First Church, or bring to life the style of entertaining when Lincoln was alive, we have indeed a fuller sense of the days whose dust first settled on those ruby glasses.

What were some of those great notions and intensities? From the days when this *was* an actual village, and Eliot and Centre a dusty four corners, this stretch of country land seemed to lure iconoclasts, men who dreamed of improving upon conventions for a just cause. The Reverend John Eliot, a longtime advocate for the Indians, led the fight for racial integration by leaving seventy-five acres of his estate for a schoolhouse for "Whites, Indians and Negroes." In 1806 a successful fur merchant, Benjamin Bussey, bought four hundred acres of land and transformed them into the walking paths and arbored summits that would become the world-renowned Arnold Arboretum. In 1890 Thomas Plante built a shoe factory and equipped it with parks, bowling alleys, a gymnasium, Saturday afternoon concerts and dances, a circulating library, and a weekly newspaper.

But I'd been hoping for more of a sense of the everyday broadcloth, for a more homely, chipped heirloom or two that might lend themselves to my life on the less provisioned shelves of civic principles today. These, however, appear to be the function of accumulation, not individual genius, of births and years and movements that resemble waves more than flashes of light. Precisely, in short, the sorts of motions that surface and settle and leave their marks in those congregations we call cities.

And a city, by the 1890s, Jamaica Plain had become. In the course of two generations, there was poverty here and need, strange new immigrants and gaps in opportunities for work and education that bore bleakly on the community's future. These new elements called not for abrupt and singular generosities but for something more considered, a public vision of a sustaining life in common.

We have arrived at an imposing yellow Georgian on Eliot Street that draws itself up as one imagines a proper grandmother would do.

"This is the home of Ellen Swallow Richards," Reiskind tells us, "the first woman graduate of MIT."

The house says nothing one way or the other about its former resident but, according to Reiskind, it was in the kitchen here that Richards spent her days, shuttling between it and the laboratory she founded at MIT. At a time when children died for want of proper hygiene and women slaved in cramped, overheated rooms, Richards lectured them on water quality and the cleanliness of their pots and pans. She dealt with the many challenges of preserving order in the impoverished kitchens of slums. Richards became known as the mother of home economics. One wonders how she would have taken the title, so domesticated, so stripped as it is of the tireless struggles in which she engaged on behalf of working girls, housewives, women of means, and the poor on streets just like her own with their many shelves and their endless demands.

A contemporary and neighbor of Richards's, Emily Greene Balch, was like Richards a regular attendee at First Church. Balch would doubtless have known about the Needle Woman's Friend Society founded by the women of the church the year she was born. An early private-nonprofit partnership, the Society employed poor local women to make clothing and linens for local families and businesses. Balch went off to Bryn Mawr, but on graduating in 1889 she returned to Jamaica Plain. To the Needle Woman's Friend Society had been added the more contemporary example of Jane Addams's Hull House in Chicago. Proudly inspired by these exemplars, Balch founded the Jamaica Plain Working Girls' Club, the community's first settlement house, to serve local factory girls.

A second settlement house soon followed, one devoted to the community's children. Like Balch, its founder, Helen Weld, was a member of the local gentry. Though she died before she could have a significant impact on the institution that would bear her name, the Helen Weld Neighborhood House went on to make educational opportunity available to Jamaica Plain's poor children through the better part of the twentieth century.

In the execution of their goals, these founders insisted upon the work of local hands. While settlement houses elsewhere were staffed by students and outsiders, "professional" volunteers, the two in Jamaica Plain were run by residents. Neighbor-to-neighbor efforts, these activists insisted, were the most effective and meaningful way to help people who lived a ten-minute walk of one another.

At a time when educated men and women were intensely global in their outlook, it was inconceivable to these women that the needs of local places should be abrogated for a loftier vantage. Always, they argued, the neighborhood was to be se-cured in its vital needs, and not least those of its women and children, before the world would be changed.

We have reached the end of our tour, in a parking lot not far from the Loring-Greenough House, where we began. It is bus-tling on this sunny Saturday morning, as folks duck into the liquor store or the bank with children in tow.

We are standing on the site of America's first independent kindergarten, Reiskind tells us. The Village School was founded by Pauline Agassiz Shaw in 1877, introducing daring and in-novative notions of children's unrecognized abilities to a rapidly urbanizing society.

Shaw was the daughter of Louis Agassiz and the wife of Quincy Adams Shaw. She'd raised her own five children in Jamaica Plain, throwing herself into making their lives as rich and stimulating as possible. To Shaw, proper child-rearing was "*the* great problem of the race"—the ultimate challenge of cul-tural continuity and strength. No amount of attention ought to be spared during this crucial stage in the development of future citizens.

Captivated by the efforts of another J.P. woman, Elizabeth Peabody, to persuade the Boston schools to adopt a transitional year between home and the rote academic rigors of grammar school, Shaw set up the Village School. The Village School was her laboratory. Based on its success, Shaw went on to finance and oversee some thirty-one other such kindergartens in the Boston schools before the school committee voted to discontinue her experiment. In time, the schoolhouse was razed to put down the blacktop on which we stand. But the young people lucky enough to be enrolled during its early years carried into adulthood Shaw's lavish sensitivity and respect for their formative environment.

Doubtless, the Village School would have evolved into a café or a gallery or printer's shop by now. But the historic marker denoting its original purpose would have remained affixed to its front, a reminder and an inspiration, rather than to a street post outside the Dunkin Donuts, where it stands, rusty and ignored above the tabloids in their battered metal boxes.

Across the street, the original houses from that era still stand—quaint capes and cottages. Into the living room of one of these, I was privileged to peer one night not long ago. A young couple was moving in, working class I would guess. Their exhausted yet hopeful faces were blind to this voyeur in the parking lot. Watching them try to mount curtain rods in the windows hours after they ought to have been asleep—the strain, their earnestness, the pleasure and the giddy uncertainty of setting up house together—stirred memories of my own first flat with the man who would become my husband.

It is possible that children will come into these lives. If so, they will learn that Mrs. Shaw's passion fared no better than her first schoolhouse, in a society increasingly committed to progress in the form of the cheap and the new. Quality kindergartens continue to be underfunded, misunderstood, marginal, a private privilege rather than a cherished public tradition.

Our tour is over. I saunter back to the lowly rocking chair, which no one else has snapped up. That its maker succeeded in winning over some child is evidenced by the care involved in preserving it intact through who knows how many domestic rearrangements, family moves, marriages, crises, and periods of disaffection.

It is an unexpected thought to have arrived at on a Saturday morning—that the stuff of history turns over and over on itself in the hands of women. It is women through the ages who not only have fastened the buttons but preserved the extra ones, who shifted the material life of the family from drawer to attic, cellar to rummage sale, and back again. The personal reinforces the public, which in time enriches the private. All turning, turning, to make a place uniquely itself.

If I take the rocker, as I am inclined to do, I will certainly adapt it to a purpose other than its original one. I do not know if its young owner was bright or dim, or whether she ever felt the benefit of Mrs. Shaw's ardent mission. I know only that she was poor and loved, and that she likely lived at a time when the women of her neighborhood conducted themselves as if the public house and its occupants merited the same care as one's favorite buttons, in the wisdom that someday this too would be the future, up for consideration in the yard sales of time. It is the quixotic nature of history that, while the new only makes us childlike, the old can make us new. I part with eight dollars and cradle it home in my arms.

PRAYING

The concept that a community can set standards, adopt values, capture conscience and become authoritative in the lives of human beings is not obvious in our culture, and it falls apart without it.
—ROBERT BELLAH ET AL., *Habits of the Heart,* 1985

THE BABY IS HOME sick with a cold, in good hands with purple crayons, and I have driven down to Hyde Square for a cup of hot coffee and a bagel at Sorella's. Though I'm usually up early, the farthest I normally venture at this hour is out to the garage, where I keep a cushion for the dog and can be assured of quiet as the sun comes up. I read in the early mornings—poetry, fragments of philosophy, things I haven't the concentration for the rest of the day. I manage, in a good hour, to approach the elemental silence of prayer.

And so, to find myself seated on a wooden bench scanning the litany of thirty-nine pancake specials for which this place is rightly famous, and conversing with the exhausted waitress who's moonlighting from a teaching job, is, well, bracing. But there comes a point in the rhythm of even the most disciplined inner life when it is good to shake up the certitudes, turn the ignition over in the aging Geo, and step into the cold of a

February morning in the attitude the ancients would have called "observance."

The streets are quiet. Except for the waitress and the short-order cook who lounges at one of the Formica tables awaiting the brunch crowd, I am alone.

I am also invisible. To observe, as I've noticed many times in unlikely hours and circumstances when I might suppose that I'd stand out most awkwardly, is to be oddly nullified. We are devotees of action in this culture, not reflection; of power more than wisdom. Two possibilities explain the transparency that seems to descend on otherwise able-bodied adults in a state of rest in the city. Either there is something in the observing stance that says, Discount me from the logic of whatever is happening; I am not a player. Or we are all invisible to one another most of the time and just don't take notice of this fact, we are so preoccupied by our own concerns.

I pay for my seat and warm comfort and step outside. Across the street a man was killed the month I moved here. The only other establishment that's open is Mike's News. Just now it admits a woman carrying an armful of roses. A red-and-white taxi idles opposite in the cold. Maybe the two are connected; maybe not. Early morning has that magic, and Sunday morning that much more. The first time I laid eyes on a real city was at daybreak on a Sunday morning. I'd ridden through the night on a cramped charter bus with my classmates and a few intrepid parents for a weekend of theater in New York. Somewhere around four in the morning, we'd fallen asleep. But as we hauled down Amsterdam into Harlem, the sudden shift in light, the closing down of sound—whatever it was—something caused me to stir. I opened my eyes. Around me on the bus sleeping bodies shifted, surfaced, and surrendered again to dream. Outside on the gray stoops of Harlem, the last and first of waking humanity were making their way past one another through the first light with a solemnity that fixed that hour forever in my heart with a special sanctity.

I knew even then that most of those we passed on our slow descent into Manhattan—weary women, the youngsters in their laps, beautiful men who strode past them without looking, and old men in jaunty caps—weren't aware of having any particular role in the hour. But there was no doubt that they were cognizant of the threshold they were crossing, bearing up yet again; that they were present for one of the great turnings in creation.

If they'd seized the opportunity for observance, they would have sung the hour, or turned it into a poem. Since that morning I've spent many hours with the city at rest, quartering myself at the entryways of her silences, among the homeless and junkies, prostitutes, and cops and those who would save them, because there is a grace and mystery to these hours that is essentially the grace and mystery—not of nature, certainly, nor of purity, nor of some grand abstraction of "city" conveyed in its architectural conceits—but of the very thing it is so hard for us often to find beautiful: man himself.

The roses and their owner reappear in Mike's doorway, and turn north on foot. And now the driver, probably a student, perhaps a lover, lowers the book that I see he's been reading and moves off. I slow my stride and swallow a breath of frigid air.

A bizarre drug transaction, had been my first thought about the pair in this neighborhood. But it proved a false assumption, a dispatch from my weekday mind with its stereotyping and thereby muddling illusions. On Sunday mornings I liken my observances to the walking meditations of pilgrims, and as usual I stand corrected by the finer capacities of the truth to shape the world in which I move if only I slow down enough to let myself actually see it.

Now, walking meditations are conventionally undertaken by monks within the confines of cloistered grounds, and a city resembles a cloister in close to nothing. But it is precisely for this reason that its hours of quietude are so necessary. Are we not the same creatures as those who rise to the cry of crows or the abbot's bell? We, too, need to see our life not merely as some frantic machine of power but as an elegant vessel of striving, talent, grace, and occasionally transcendent purpose.

And so on this morning when nature and a good part of the animal kingdom are at rest, it isn't a marbled walkway that I see, but a few faithful old women on pensions hunched over leashes waiting for their companions to do the right thing. And not manicured herb gardens but shabby windburnt grass on old city lots. It is the black paperboy, off-loading weighty papers from the front seat of a rusted Toyota while his girlfriend dozes under a blanket in the back, and men in frayed sneakers who gather cans from the Dumpster and keep where they can to the thin patches of sunlight.

But—and this is the great secret shared between invisibility and faith—what matters to my understanding is the same thing that matters on the mountaintops of France or to the Trappists

of Kentucky. The setting is immaterial. To be at rest is to observe the bones of God's work through man in the world laid
bare. To be at rest is to see with clarified vision. And this vision
forces me to contemplate not what I am meant to *do* with my
days in this place on earth, but what I am meant to *be*.

To what, here and now, am I to be faithful?

History's great city dwellers—Jews, Christians, and Muslims—
mandated the Sabbath as a matter of law. One day every week,
the land, the work animals, and all civil institutions were to
rest. Weeds were not to be pulled, accounts not to be done;
cleaning, cooking, buying, selling—even reading—were to de-
sist to allow for the more subtle action of the soul.

Even granting that life may have been simpler in those days,
more consonant with the tempos of nature and hence the necessary counterpoint of activity and rest, this was the kind of
solution my mother would have approved of: it implicated all
and forgave none. The problem of the human psyche and its
defiant will is an eternal one, best met head-on with consistency, on pain of ostracism.

Worship helped to focus the intent of this twenty-four-hour
period. It was the centering vehicle without which rest would
have grown wanton, desacralized—mere wasteful leisure. Not
only was worship a valuable discipline, a reminder of the need
to slow down and to hear once again the ancient teachings. If
it was good, and the devout were in a condition to receive,
worship could move one closer to the truth about oneself and
the mystery of one's being on earth. It sustained neighbors,

businessmen, and families in a shared language of norms, imparting a sense that the sacred was a matter of common stewardship.

Churches stand open up and down Centre Street as I make my way. Behind me are the storefront Spanish Iglesia de Dios, and its more prosperous neighbor, the Fellowship Church of God, wedged between an ATM outlet and a fashion store. Pentecostal yields to Baptist, which in turn yields to Catholic along the Latin spectrum of Centre. Somewhere past Hyde Square the order reverses: First Baptist, First Church Unitarian Universalist, and St. Thomas are primarily white congregations, with an Episcopal and Congregational church flung off on lovely hilltops a few blocks away. There used to be more, of course, here as elsewhere, and the people involved in the rituals of worship back then doubtless worked hard. But what of their counterparts today, and the work of congregations in such vastly altered times? Most Americans assume that city dwellers just don't go to church anymore. But they would be wrong, in this neighborhood anyway.

The red doors of First Church are flung open, and to judge from the activity at the entrance on Eliot Street, the nursery is doing a brisk business. Youngsters careen around the tall wrought-iron gate, delighted to see one another, and vanish within the heavy doors of the parish house. I hoist open the solid inner doors to the sanctuary and step inside.

The organ is playing Bach's "O Welt, ich muss dich lassen." An old woman in steel rims hands me a bulletin, and I sidle into one of the original box pews toward the back. The austere purity of Unitarian spaces never fails to move me. Their white walls and eggshell windows still successfully translate the vision of those latter-day Puritans, of an attainable, transporting place within, of grace, even in this late, roiling century.

Parishioners are prompt. They are people I recognize from the streets, shops, and parks around town. They are young and old, parents who tiptoe through from the nursery, and single middle-aged women—the same crop of Christians you'd find at a country church, except that we are probably dressed more casually in work boots, old blazers, and bargain-store gear. One has the sense from the greetings that the people here see one another frequently, are "family" in a certain sense. That this is not, in other words, a place for show.

The rector, Terry Burke, moves back and forth, checking his notes at a small lectern and adjusting the altar table. A slight man with thick glasses and a graying beard, he occasionally bends to greet a parishioner in a manner both informal and gentle. At eleven exactly, he lights a white candle next to a vase of snow-white tulips, and the service begins, with a spiritual and a reading of Psalm 26.

Today, the third Sunday in Lent, is special. In lieu of a sermon, the parish's poetry group, which has met every Saturday morning for more than two years, is going to read some of their work. But before this we are saying the Lord's Prayer, some fifty voices strong, and joining in three verses of "Abide With Me."

When Terry Burke arrived here in 1983 on a part-time, three-month assignment from the district Unitarian Universalist office downtown, First Church averaged Sunday attendance of sixteen, all of them over the age of eighty. The church hadn't had a full-time minister in thirteen years. The physical plant was in desperate need of repair—so much so that the minuscule congregation used the church proper only on major holidays. The rest of the time they met in a room behind the stage in the parish house.

The morning Burke preached his first sermon, it snowed. Only thirteen people showed up to greet him.

Membership today stands at over four hundred, while the nursery and Sunday school average eighty children each week. There isn't a day, and hardly an evening, when the parish house isn't in full swing. One group is studying the Peloponnesian War; there's an ongoing women's spirituality group, and a meditation group that meets each Sunday before regular service.

In a way, the church reflects the community. It is urbane and progressive. But it is more than that, because even the most tolerant civic place doesn't offer those niches for the soul that this neighborhood church does. Burke has turned it into a haven of solace and fellowship, a place where people in the neighborhood, in a secular time, can come to be whole.

When he arrived, he knew that to tap the spiritual energies out there, he needed to open the church's doors. That first year was the twentieth anniversary of Martin Luther King, Jr.'s, March on Washington. When asked if First Church could be used for a speak-out in honor of the occasion, he readily assented. An international tour of children war survivors wanted to make First Church one of their northeastern stops. Burke agreed. When a gay and lesbian group approached him to hold a monthly dinner in the parish house, Burke hesitated briefly: he couldn't assent to alcohol on the premises.

"They were so thrilled to have this restriction put on the event," he tells me, "because so much of the gay scene revolves around the downtown bars. This actually enabled them to have the alternative kind of event they'd had in mind." A contra dance group requested use of the church on Tuesday nights. Artists came. Would First Church open its lobby for exhibitions during Open Studios weekend?

Meanwhile, Burke continued preparing his sermons and entering a sanctuary each Sunday morning where the numbers were barely budging. He was patient. He was still being paid to work only part-time. People were holding back, waiting to see "if this was real, if it was going to last." He was a man of faith.

And slowly First Church grew. Weekday visitors began coming to Sunday services. They were mostly forty-somethings who saw in the decentralized Unitarian faith and in Burke himself both the safety to search for God without the more rigid constraints of conservative orthodoxies and the chance to build a church with a social agenda that matched their own.

Burke embraced them, but he did so with the conviction of his faith. Church, first and foremost, was about one's relation to God, he would tell them. The center of life at First Church was the act of Sunday worship.

"People really need a spiritual language to articulate what their experience is," he says. "And you need to know that language in some depth. My approach is that you do that as a worshipping community."

The language at First Church is, in Burke's words, "Judeo-

Christian-theistic." They follow the Christian church calendar, read psalms, sing the old hymns, and talk about daily prayer.

"Many people in the congregation are in human service work and 'alternative' work," Burke tells me. "Legal aid lawyers, alcohol counselors. They might be nurses and doctors, but they work in inner-city clinics. They're already doing what I'd call ministries."

There is a tendency for such congregations to turn church into a spiritual extension of work. "I say to them, 'It's very important to be involved in peace and justice issues, but you need to have a personal spiritual discipline that you do every day that deepens your spiritual life and connects you more deeply with God.' "

In other words: prayer. Prayer, and Sunday worship.

"Worship is the way you grow into God," Burke tells them, adding, "The church is a meeting house. People come in, you encounter people who are different, and you encounter all the issues of the world. But in our time it's also a sanctuary, a place where you can try to connect with God and you can try and understand what it means to be a human being, and you don't have to follow the conventional wisdom or the norms of the world outside the door."

Granola gospel this wasn't, but people bought it. They came, brought friends, had their children baptized. For his part, Burke has shown them the ways in which the many modalities of the sacred can grow from a center of prayer and scripture into vital community. The result has the feeling of a many-layered dialogue, a mingling of cultural expression, social engagement, and sanctuary that is still intimate enough to be "about" particular souls.

It is time for the poems. The membership grows still. One by one, parishioners brave the sound of their small private voices amplified in the venerable space. These are poems about grief: the pain of raising a son in divorce; of hearing a grandson's trumpet performing "Amazing Grace" at his grandfather's funeral; words spoken to a child dead in the womb.

When it is over, no one stirs. Then the organist begins the first phrases of "Amazing Grace," and we stand, dab our eyes, and sing our hearts out.

Soon the service is over. Congregants course up the aisles and embrace the poets. The grieving young woman is still brimming with tears. Every one of them, like us, has been touched and won't forget this morning anytime soon.

I step back out into the street, intending to go home. But instead I stroll down to the hardware store. I don't need anything so badly. Maybe I'll find a bag of clothespins or a packet of seeds.

I am with the city, but I am no longer alone: not the way I was before I went to church. There's a line outside Pinardi's. People clutch their *Globes* and Sunday *Times*es and hope that a table will open up soon. We are workers here, not at the top of any ladders, but the people who keep the engines of the city going. We need to rise early, and we come home late, and most of us need to make every penny count, and for most of us, it doesn't quite stretch. Yet we continue nevertheless to have faith in ourselves and in the process of rising each Monday to set our efforts to whatever employments will have them, pouring coffee for one another, selling shoes, making beautiful frames, planting trees, listening.

We know that the peeling paint and tired condition of certain storefronts—the stuff that makes outsiders pass us by without a second glance—will come and go, but that what stays and matters is the animating humanity of this place. A hand-scrawled note in one shop window reads: "Nobody has ever measured how much the heart can hold."

All of this makes me grateful. It is the imagination and the toil of the people I live among that make my life what it is, valued, challenged, "held" in a vital web of meaning.

"To live and die with the neighborhood." The phrase has stayed with me ever since Terry Burke used it in a conversation a while back to describe the purpose of an urban neighborhood church. "God is a reality," he told me. "God isn't just an abstraction. It's something you walk with on the streets."

Maybe this, right here, is the gospel of the common life. It is a noble calling, I see this morning, to keep fidelity between one's work and one's neighbors and one's soul. Each implies the other. Each informs the other. In ancient societies to be a good citizen was to be a pious one. It was to walk in observance.

I buy a bag of clothespins and step back into the street. Some of the late departers from church have straggled down. We smile. When I moved here, I didn't expect that my quest for community would lead me to craftsmen, much less drug dealers or humble Xerox-shop managers, or that a world of Mondays would come to echo the wisdom of the Psalms. But coming into the heart of a place is learning to see its indwelling spirits. Once you know how to look, they are everywhere.

2 / COMMUNITY

If there are not habituated patterns of work, play, grieving, and celebration designed to enable people to live well in a place, then those
people will have at best a limited capacity for being public with one
another. Conversely, where such inhabitory practices are being nur-
tured, the foundation for public life is also being created or maintained.

—DANIEL KEMMIS, *Community and the Politics of Place*, 1990

Here is a challenge: community is the product not of tradition but of
personal responsibility, yours to build or destroy.

—HENRY GLASSIE, *Passing the Time in Ballymenone*, 1982

*MEN AND WOMEN who choose to live like citizens are the
elements of hope and sustenance in any community, and the
place that lacks them can hardly be called whole. But what
we've learned in Jamaica Plain is that for a community to be
healthy, the choices we make about our lives as individuals
aren't enough. Our caring about our small corner of the city,
whether it begins in a shared garden, the condition of an apartment building, a favorite shop, or a local salsa band, begs for
more enduring form. And so we've searched for ways to give
some permanence to what we love.*

*Casual contact and a sense of place are continually intensi-
fying into projects of an economic and political nature. Over
and over again we are learning how to be creatively and effectively public with one another. It is a never-ending process, this
grassroots democracy, and the day it ends, genuine community
life ends with it.*

There is a lot of theory floating around these days about "community" and its continued possibility in American culture. Some say that we've gone too far as a society in the direction of "process" democracy, allowing lobbying and savvy at working the system to rob communities of substantive debate, or even the venues in which to debate. Well-organized interests win the day, leaving the complex grassroots communities around them leached of resources, energy, and the wherewithal to withstand predatory social and economic pressures from without. These procedural critics argue that without some "thing," some social contract that transcends narrow special interests and holds a community in common trust, our form of democracy with its procedural bias will always run over community, and values will always lose to brinksmanship.

Preserving a healthy political ecology has proven America's most daunting task. The lessons of Jamaica Plain teach that it must begin in the small places. To the extent that we work as a community, we have managed over a twenty-five-year period to generate patterns of engagement, defense, and broadly shared values. Many of the people who began this work a quarter century ago—people like Christine Cooper at the pond and Terry Burke at First Church—are still around. This is important. We need them to uphold our sense of where we've come from. But over the years new voices have added themselves to the conversation as well; new talents, challenges, and perspectives have contributed. Together they have taught us that a healthy urban neighborhood, indeed any healthy community, is well served by—and may even be dependent upon—the elements of stability, residential density, change, and diversity.

Today Jamaica Plain is a crazy quilt of groups, distinct

traditions, and differentiated residential neighborhoods that overlap and crisscross one another in hundreds of different ways. We have learned to come together in crisis. We have created our own brand of public rituals. We meet on a thriving Main Street and in homegrown associations. The result is a place where people care enough to talk to one another and listen, to take positions and argue, and out of respect for the preservation of our common life, to agree to live by the consequent resolutions. In this way our common language, our ways and norms, has been sufficiently and broadly developed to stand its ground against process run amok.

Born of "process," our distinguishing ways have taken on the more enduring forms of principle and history, enabling us to call a halt to what is counterfeit or bullying until the requisite terms of the common good are reestablished. We have learned to be effective in the face of large government, to defend ourselves alike against invasive plans and neglect.

A community is a multilayered and densely textured organism. In events remembered, challenges overcome, and the passage of time itself, its characters find their place and the understanding of their purpose. It takes longevity and commitment to raise a healthy place. If the first stories in this book illustrate aspects of citizenship that significantly improve the quality of the common life, those that follow speak to the ways in which our shared language and ways have evolved. Drawn from our contemporary narrative, they are intended as parables. For while they concern very real events that have been crucial in forming the uncommon life we have achieved in Jamaica Plain, they are also exemplary of work that could be done in living communities everywhere.

CULTIVATING

AN OTHERWISE FORGOTTEN VISITOR passing through Jamaica Plain in the early 1800s was moved to christen it "the Eden of America." He wasn't exactly the first to seize on this conceit, but he wasn't far off either. There were the massive drifts of rhododendron overlooking the pond, of course, and the greens of the Arnold Arboretum. Had he arrived a century later, he would have found his fancy confirmed in less obvious quarters, in the pocket gardens of the working class.

From one end of Centre Street to the other, housewives coaxed roses and marigolds from early morning until dusk. Along tree-lined avenues, back patches were given over to tomatoes and grapes and raspberries. On Sunday afternoons whole families would sit out on their porches and bask in the tidy exuberance of well-tended sod. Long before it was trendy, Jamaica Plainers of all classes had made this art a form of public pride.

All, that is, except those families who lived beneath the elevated train that rattled down Washington Street from early morning until late at night on its backside-of-the-city run. In this part of town the sun didn't even seem to shine. Each spring young Winky Cloherty used to watch her grandmother doggedly press her ailanthuses into the soil out in front of the old triple-decker with a sort of resigned stupefaction.

"Don't worry, Mrs. Naruszewicz," the neighborhood plumber was fond of humoring her. "All this will all be coming down someday soon." And he'd gesture to the ribs of relentless steel.

Winky didn't know how many times she'd heard this, but she had no intention of waiting to see the day. She planned to marry and make a life as far from Jamaica Plain as possible, on an uncluttered suburban street, with a spotless lawn, a lav off the kitchen, and a rec room for the kids.

Meanwhile, she always had the penny candy store and Pelham Drug's soda fountain, where she went to escape the perpetual twilight. There was no shame attached to stepping into town from Egleston Square. Our Lady of Lourdes held its own with the best of St. Mary of the Angels and Blessed Sacrament, the CYOs, and the mission drives. Life in the forties and fifties was of a piece. The immigrant and second-generation Irish, Italian, Greek, and Ukrainian families who dwelled in its two- and three-family homes made good neighbors. Most of the men worked in trades. The women stayed home, forming a sort of cadre of motherhood whose foot soldiers saw to it that no one else's children did anything they wouldn't tolerate from their own.

No one was rich, but nearly everyone made enough to keep a three-mile strip street of merchants—grocers, shoe sellers, clothiers, and furniture makers—flourishing. During the school year, sent off in the morning with the day's "penny for Baby Jesus," Winky and all her friends would see to it that the candy man thrived. And after school there were always scouts or Junior Achievement, the pond and its parks, and the public library story hour and puppet shows to keep her occupied until dinner. Come the long days of a city summer the likes of she and Christine Cooper could loiter in front of the window at Louie's Meat Market and hope to get an apple from the stack of produce with which he lured the housewives in. Or they could make macramé bracelets when the Parks Department activities truck came through, or take a day trip out to a farm under the auspices of the Helen Weld Neighborhood House, returning with cucumbers and peas after a day of fresh air and weeding. And never far from view was her grandmother to organize useful garden projects and, on special occasions, an ice cream at the Pelham.

Before Winky knew it, she was donning plaid skirts and studying at the local state college, like a lot of her friends, to become a kindergarten teacher. When classes got out each day, she took the bus back to Our Lady of Lourdes Church and her part-time job as a CYO counselor. Charlie Cloherty was working there, too, earning his way through college.

Winky'd known Charlie for years. He'd been one of the altar boys at the early Mass. Now they began to walk home together and talk. Charlie had grown up on tree-lined Montebello Road a few blocks away, in a house bought when his Irish-born grandfather had saved enough to make the down payment. Charlie shared not only a good part of Winky's past but her hopes for the future as well. He wanted to get out of the city. The future wasn't here, he agreed. He wanted to settle down somewhere green, and raise a family in a home of his own.

The dream, the brightness, and the hope were dazzling, and within a few short months, Charlie had asked Winky to marry him. From that moment on, the streets of town faded like old wallpaper.

One day while she was at work, Winky heard about a community meeting at the Neighborhood House. Like any self-respecting Jamaica Plainer, moving or not, she was curious. On the way home, she decided to drop in.

That evening in the summer of 1964, members of the city's Redevelopment Authority stood at the podium and discussed plans to dismantle the elevated train. A master plan to this effect had been around for nearly fifteen years, the speaker told the modest assemblage of locals. Executed, it would bring Boston into the modern era. An eight-lane highway would circle Boston's central district and connect at both ends with a federally funded interstate that would eventually link Maine to Florida. Plans for the Inner Belt, as the eight-lane city section was being called, were impressive and ambitious. And Jamaica Plain would play a small part, in carrying several miles of the highway into neighboring Roxbury, where a five-story interchange would siphon off local commuters.

It was the first time in Jamaica Plain memory that the state was inserting itself so decisively into the community's affairs. Winky was impressed. And like almost everyone else who listened that evening, delighted. Though she wouldn't be around to enjoy them, her grandmother's flowers at last would see the light of day.

She and Charlie soon packed their wedding gifts into Charlie's car and drove to Warren, Michigan. The apartment complex they settled into was brand-new and up-to-the-minute; the lawns perfectly manicured, the paint fresh. It seemed too good to be true. They started their house search, scouring development after development of much the same: tidy brick ranches and perfect green sod on gently wending lanes. At last they put a down payment on a place. The dream they'd waited so long for was about to come true.

But as the days went by, the dream grew dimmer. When she took out the trash, Winky never saw another human being. Dogs were a rarity; hardly even a bird deigned to light on one of their trees. There were no tricycles in the driveways, no sweaty neighbor out holding hoses just waiting for a good yarn to turn up. She began to consider the possibility that the dream wasn't all that it was cracked up to be.

"We didn't grow up in Valhalla," she would say thirty years later. "But people knew one another, people talked to one another. People walked! Out there you had to drive everywhere. I think we could have died in the house, and we still wouldn't have known anybody."

They lasted a year, before they decided to return home.

Back in Jamaica Plain, the state's highway plan was getting under way. Few in the community had grasped from the early meetings that the concrete and neon would have to be preceded by the eradication of homes and businesses, playgrounds and streets. The neighborhood that Winky grew up in would have to give way to a transportation system that its displaced citizens would rarely use.

Winky and Charlie returned to find that savvy property owners across the entire backside of town had become absentee landlords. FOR SALE signs in the windows of small groceries went begging because the banks, too, had caught the drift. When they found a house up on a rise overlooking Egleston, a good mile from the proposed demolition, they were turned down for a $13,000 mortgage from the local Boston Five Cents Savings, despite Charlie's government job and extended family ties in the neighborhood. The bulldozers hadn't arrived yet, but the mental demolition was well under way.

Winky felt violated, betrayed—and mobilized. When it came to questions of community, her experience in Michigan had radically shifted her compass. To her prodigal soul, roots and continuity were far more important than showy beauty—and certainly more important than efficiency and convenience. That fall of 1967, she attended yet another meeting at the Neighborhood House. This time a man named Jim Morey spoke. Morey had been working in Cambridge for a year with residents who opposed the Inner Belt there. He was paid by a nonprofit organization called Urban Planning Aid, set up by the American Friends Service Committee to help citizens groups who couldn't afford to hire political experts but who needed their skills to deal with the semiautonomous government agencies and authorities that had emerged since World War II.

That evening Morey told those who'd come out that there were alternatives to the eight-lane monstrosity that would soon shear off a section of their town. If they were willing to put some effort into researching and then lobbying for a less intrusive highway design, he and others would support them with technical assistance and strategic advice.

Winky trusted him, and opposition to the Inner Belt in Jamaica Plain was born that night. The group called themselves the Jamaica Plain Expressway Committee. And Winky became one of its most ardent foot soldiers.

While some researched alternative road designs, her job was to drum up support among the churches. It was familiar turf. Week after week, she sat down with local pastors who'd known her since before she strapped on her first pair of Mary Janes, and tried to persuade them to allow her committee to make presentations to their Holy Name societies and ladies' sodalities about the possibility of depressing the highway and reducing its scale enough to salvage the community.

However, Winky discovered her greatest support among the new arrivals in town. They were young couples with children, like her and Charlie, who were committed to putting down roots in the city and wanted an intact community in which to do so. The newcomers weren't to be found in the churches and felt no fealty to the old political ward tradition. If the old rules didn't work, they believed they needed to take the process into their own hands.

The bulldozers arrived. The wrecking balls, the flatbeds, and dump trucks came rolling down the shadow of the elevated. And wherever they came, they pushed anything that stood in their path out of their way. Walls and trees collapsed in their maws. For the local opposition, the battle became one of time.

The Jamaica Plain Expressway Committee soon began to meet sympathetic soul mates along the entire proposed path of the highway from Roxbury to Cambridge. It included urban residents as well as suburbanites increasingly concerned with the environmental effect of the road on vulnerable wetlands. Throughout the following fall the groups were in constant contact with one another, crafting what they hoped would be an unassailable public relations assault on the statehouse. And in January they carried it off.

Thousands of residents from each of the affected neighborhoods came together within spitting distance of the capitol. They demanded a moratorium on highway construction and the demolition of homes. They asked the governor for a personal review of the highway plan.

The newly inaugurated governor, eager to mollify the crowds, agreed. But only in part. The 1948 state master plan would be revisited. But the bulldozing would continue. Several days later, Winky flew to Washington. There she listened to congressional testimony from people like herself all over the country as they described the devastating effects on their quality of life of inner-city highway projects similar to the Massachusetts Highway master plan.

She returned to Jamaica Plain galvanized. "We're making a mistake if we settle for a depressed road," she told people as soon as she could catch her breath. "We've got to stop the whole thing!"

The Jamaica Plain Expressway Committee pulled out the stops. They deluged state reps with postcard campaigns. They worked the back channels to the federal highway department.

Two years of demolition lay all around them. Weary and dispirited, they waited for the governor's task force report, a long eleven months in the coming.

Finally in January 1970 it was finished. That night the governor went on television and in a ten-minute address declared a freeze on property taking along the Jamaica Plain and Roxbury part of the project, and a partial moratorium on the rest of the project, pending the results of a restudy.

By the time the bulldozers were stopped, they'd demolished more than seven hundred homes, three hundred businesses, and an intricate organism of roots and tendrils that had nourished generations of neighbors in the Eden of America. Our Lady of Lourdes survived, as did Winky's grandmother's home, but from where Winky stood not far away, she could see nothing but desolation. Eight miles long and a half mile wide, two thousand acres in all had been carved off the backside of Jamaica Plain and down through the city's core.

The remnants of the earlier life were strewn everywhere. Doll parts and curtain rods stuck up from the dirt, picture frames and old bills lay scattered half-buried in ash. The stranger who'd found in the old neighborhood a verdant Eden had been thinking of its flora. Now that it was destroyed, people knew that the story had always been more complex than that. A certain innocence, it was true, had been lost; but more important, an ineffable integrity had disappeared. Over the course of generations, Jamaica Plain had accrued its own habits, traditions, and norms. People of different backgrounds and means had learned how to coexist well with one another and with the natural abundance around them, in ways that had come to constitute an indigenous local culture.

As Winky surveyed the scorched earth on a winter morning in 1970, she knew that nothing would bring that world back. The land would stand raw for the better part of a decade, a wasteland on the edge of the ghetto. No one needed to be told what this implied. The state had learned its lesson, too. The old ward system had not delivered the docile electorate it had expected when it began. Whatever became of the destroyed neighborhoods that were now being euphemized as "the Southwest Corridor," officials realized that considerable room would have to be made for the community's own will.

If Christine Cooper's pond-reclamation project ushered in the flowering of pedestrian life again in Jamaica Plain, its roots were first set down in the ravaged scene that a group of pioneers discovered in the early seventies when they moved in.

The first time Peter Rosenbaum made his way down to the unreconstructed corridor land just two blocks from his house on Clive Street, a group of kids from the opposite side of the tracks had recently set fire to a swing set that some mother had put out there for the children to play with. Peter, a gentle, bearded lumberjack of a man, wasn't surprised. He'd just returned from two years' teaching in inner-city Philadelphia, and he knew something of the frustration and rage of the children that no one in society wanted.

On this particular morning, however, his interest in this strip of wasteland was less sociological than personal. He was twenty-four and between teaching stints in Philly, and he was taking courses at the Harvard School of Education, about to enter a doctoral program. While a part of him hardly felt ready to own the massive six-bedroom Victorian he and his new wife, Femke, were considering just a few blocks from where he stood, it was almost too good to turn down.

At $21,000 the house had four times the space they could afford in Cambridge. And its spaciousness would allow the life-style both he and Femke were looking for. As a Harvard undergraduate, he'd dabbled in radical politics. But in the end he'd decided that they weren't for him. Instead he commenced an ardent search for ways in which institutions could be challenged effectively from within the limits of the law. And except for a year's postgraduate traveling fellowship, during which he'd hitchhiked to Afghanistan and back, Peter had remained true to this commitment. His academic work at Harvard was focused on exploring ways in which games and play could be introduced into school curricula to better help children, particularly underprivileged children, learn. Both he and his wife, an elementary-school art teacher, suspected that there were many kids in J.P. like the ones who'd destroyed the swing set to whom a home like the one on Clive Street might offer a sense of belonging.

In 1974 Jamaica Plain was a community in search of itself, and this suited the Rosenbaums as well. There were plenty of issues to get involved in, not the least being the disposition of the arid corridor land. Already they'd begun to meet people who were trying to make the community a better place to live. There were John Rowse and Sue Naimark around the corner in a triple-decker on Paul Gore. John had started a local building materials cooperative to encourage the rehabilitation of the posthighway deteriorated housing. Sue was just twenty. She'd found her way east from Michigan to attend architecture school, but after taking a hands-on housing construction course that John offered at the Jamaica Plain Agassiz School, she decided to stay on in J.P. and form a local carpentry and painting business. And there was Michael Simon, fresh from Southern California, who cycled everywhere rather than use a car and earned his living helping people renovate houses. Slug, as Peter was sometimes called, liked the energy he felt whenever he and Femke came across the river to visit.

Peter's relations were telling him that buying in Jamaica Plain was risky, a marginal investment at best. Housing prices were continuing to drop. All he and Femke had to do was look around: the shells of torched properties stood everywhere, full of who knew what. Just because a few intrepid souls had set up house in an urban war zone didn't mean that he had to join the crusade.

But as he turned to go on this morning, Peter took one last look at the no-man's-land, his mind already made up. If it was risky, he felt, so much the better. In his mind's eye he was already seeing parks and playgrounds, and a place where his passions for social justice and nature might find a common home of their own.

They moved that August. In the evenings when Peter returned from work, Femke would go out to one of the many meetings being held around the neighborhood. The most colorful of all of them, she soon discovered, were the Station Area Task Force meetings. In the wake of the highway debacle, the state had created a Transportation Planning Review Board. The group, comprising local residents as well as professionals, had recommended using part of the corridor land for a greatly modernized subway line and a parallel commuter rail. The question was what to do with the rest. And this was where it got interesting.

The meetings were wild and raucous affairs, full of the kind of high political theater Femke hadn't seen since the sixties. Up at the front of the room chairing the meetings was Ruth Parker of the conservative Civic Improvement League, and in their metal folding chairs were the usual cadre of her considerable constituency. These conservatives wanted to return Jamaica Plain to the community it had once been—working class, churchgoing, and white—and they saw constructing market-rate, rather than low-income, housing on the burnt-out land as the way to accomplish this.

Peter, unable to stay away, soon joined Femke. They'd often run into some of the other newcomers there. People like Sue and John and Michael routinely turned out. They watched and cheered on a local woman they'd gotten to know who always had the moxie to take on Ruthie and her group. Winky Cloherty was the real article. She was smart, plugged in, a genuine grassroots progressive. She wanted to see the land around the stations turned over to low-income housing as well as desperately needed recreational facilities and parks where the seeds of new community could be planted and coaxed.

To the conservatives like Ruth, these were buzz phrases for integration and economic diversity. And often the evenings disintegrated into shouting matches between the two groups and preemptive exits. The occasional drunk was on hand to ham it up, and hovering somewhere on the periphery was the state project manager, whose hapless job it was to protect the new political process of "inclusivity" and encourage the factions to arrive at some kind of consensus.

But Slug often left the meetings with a sense of wry empathy for his fellow residents in this benighted part of town. Just about the only thing that was patently clear to everyone who sat through the hours of vitriol was just how precious their bone of contention was to them. These people loved their place. And at this point in its history, its richest asset was a rubble heap. Less obvious most nights, the true asset was they themselves, the souls who were willing to continue showing up week after week to endure what unquestionably was going to be the longest and most wrenching conversation any of them had ever had about community.

Peter's family was growing quickly, first one child, then two more. The children were getting old enough to roam the neighborhood streets on their own, and still there had been no resolution of the problem of the corridor land just a few blocks away, in large part because the subway construction hadn't made it this far down the line yet.

One day Slug went out walking the route he'd taken several years earlier when deciding whether to move to J.P. He spotted several forms in the middle distance hugging the earth. It looked as if someone had set up a small encampment, an outpost along this dispiriting frontier. Squatters had come and gone before; it wasn't unusual to stumble on a vagrant here or there. But as Slug got closer, he was surprised. It was Sue Naimark. She was knee-deep in dirt.

The worst of the job was behind her, she told him. She and about twenty others had pulled car parts and tires and God knew what else from this acre in the middle of the few fossil walls and foundations that remained.

The place, she confided, had been full of "crap. I kept expecting to find bodies."

Not far away was a mound of fresh topsoil. Behind it, what from a distance had appeared to be a tent proved now to be a greenhouse-in-progress. When she wasn't hauling away bags of trash, Sue, with her carpentry skills, was supervising its construction.

The idea was to supply local gardeners with organic seedlings, she told him. Around the greenhouse, on the land where they stood, residents of the surrounding streets could "lease" plots in which to grow their own food.

Sue had big plans. Local children could learn the rudiments of gardening, and the elderly residents in the neighborhood's nursing homes could get some tips on nutrition. The garden could be used for demonstrations and teaching. Until the state decided what to do with it, this patch of greenspace would be a place where the newcomers and old-timers of the neighborhood could gather on common ground. They were calling themselves the Southwest Corridor Community Farm.

Slug gazed out. As far as the eye could see gaped a scorched-earth scene of toppled buildings and uncleared lots, an old rail embankment, and in the far distance, the cranes and backhoes of the next assault of construction. But here under a hot spring sun, folks young and old, black, white, Asian, and Latino, were hauling away rocks and talking flowers. But they were at a crossroads, Sue told him. The small CETA grant that had financed the clearing operation was about to run out. To continue work on the greenhouse and begin actual cultivation, an infusion of local volunteers was needed.

Slug needed little goading. He joined the board of the fledgling farm, took a plot, and voted Sue its first director.

The neighbors eyed all this with caution. Was this a drug cult, or, worse, a commune? When Sue knocked on their doors with the hope of explaining the project, they remained closed.

But finally one day Sue hit pay dirt. Behind one particular house on Chestnut, rose vines wound three stories up to a trellised porch. She rang the bell and was greeted like a lost daughter by the Berardis and the Rizzos, Italian-born neighbors who'd been squatting on an abutting piece of open ghetto land since they'd arrived in America. They raised rabbits and made wine from the cast-off grapes they collected from behind the Hi Lo Grocery every fall, and they had a compost pile that nourished enough tomatoes to keep them in carbonara all winter long. Any trouble from poachers, they assured Sue, would see the barrel of the old shotgun they kept on hand—that was how family they felt toward her and her new farm.

One day soon after this, a Cuban tomato farmer who worked at a candy factory in Cambridge brought his Italian wife down to the farm. A Honduran woman showed up wanting a flower garden, and stayed. Soon several African-American families who lived in the projects came looking for plots. Slowly word got around.

But more than any other segment of the neighborhood, it was the children who brought the farm to life that first growing season. Whenever time hung heavy—and it did often in this neighborhood of diminished hopes—they would come to hang out and follow Sue on her rounds. They accompanied her to the greenhouse to water seedlings, up to the hardware store

for tomato stakes, and back and forth along the rows of carefully laid-out beds.

The plots were beginning to offer stripes of brilliant green.
Basil and carrots and cilantro pushed up from this former
graveyard of tires. Squash turned orange, and lilies started to
drop. And before anyone knew it, it was time for the harvest.

The next spring, forty-odd people came asking for plots. A
Colombian biologist moved into the greenhouse to experiment
with the sustainability of various greens through New England
winters. The Suffolk County Cooperative Extension Service began to visit and advise gardeners on organic pest control and
other problems. With monies from a Community Development
Block Grant that was also paying her salary, Sue was able to
hire an education coordinator to run programs for children,
helping them cultivate their own plots and learn the rudiments
of husbandry, as well as classes for the local senior citizens,
who were now gardening in the greenhouse once a week.

Meanwhile, the community kept coming, planting, weeding,
and reaping. The farm had become a symbol of everything that
government bureaucracy wasn't—responsive, creative, idiosyn-
cratic, and local. The gardeners were one of the most diverse
groups anywhere in the city of Boston. People of all ages, col-
ors, educational levels, and classes gathered each weekend and
often in the early evenings to work side by side, hoeing their
rows, showing off their hard-won labors to one another—and,
increasingly, staying.

From the pitchers of lemonade and canned beer they
brought to keep cool while they worked, it was a short leap to
music and fried chicken. On warm summer evenings late in the

seventies, a stranger driving down Lamartine Street began to see small groups clustered here and there among the stands of corn, their rakes and spades laid aside. Community "work days" took on the character of block parties. Late in the morning, farm members would show up to repair the common walks, rebuild compost bins, and prune and clear. Women on welfare would bring potluck dishes to set beside the offerings of young doctors. Someone would bring a grill, the rest their best home cooking, and the day would wend toward sundown with the conviviality of an old-time barbecue, as the sun dipped into the vacant moonscape to the west.

Slug had never lost sight of the heavy equipment that was making its inexorable way down the corridor. Each day he observed its advance with greater ambivalence. If the farm had transfigured an acre of land, it had also begun to change his life. Each morning he still donned office clothes and arrived at his desk at the commission. But the days found him thinking more deeply about the farm and its welfare once the steam rollers and the politics of place finally arrived at its raspberry-hedge perimeter.

A little-used section of land adjacent to the active plots had sat idle since the farm began. By anyone's reckoning it was needless surplus and a fallow, overgrown mess besides. Now Slug began to lobby at board meetings for an orchard on the site. It seemed at first just one of his mercurial enthusiasms. They already had their hands full. But when he persisted, they finally agreed. What did they have to lose? Soon apple, pear, and apricot trees, berry bushes, and currants added their bounty to the farm's burgeoning vegetable patch.

One day not long after this, Leroy Stoddard appeared. Leroy was fresh from Maine, a frank-talking sandy blonde who'd gotten his hands into the soil of a good-sized home garden at the end of his days organizing poor rural families who needed better housing. He was interested in the job of farm director. The timing couldn't have been better: Sue, having proved in four short years that an urban farm was a viable enterprise, was ready to return to housing issues in the city's poorer neighborhoods.

It didn't take long to see that Leroy had been a gift sent from the garden gnomes. The greenhouse still produced a crop of organic seedlings each spring, but its annual profits of $10,000 were insufficient to pay for the farm's total operation. Volunteer farm members continued to improve the environs of the farm itself. They organized street cleanups and actively promoted a food cooperative, and a farmer's market in nearby Hyde Square, where low-income neighbors could buy fresh produce each Saturday.

But Leroy saw the farm's potential role in bigger terms. What had begun as a very localized vision of neighborhood and nature in an urban setting had extended its influence to a broader segment of the Jamaica Plain community. Now residents from other sections had begun to contact the farm, asking for assistance in starting community gardens of their own. Leroy hit on the idea of making a business out of the promotion and care of community gardens.

It proved a brilliantly successful stratagem. Beginning in 1982 with five small lots scattered around Jamaica Plain, a paid farm staff drawn from around the community mowed and trimmed, repaired fences, supplied and maintained signs, walking paths, and benches for the gardens, and provided lots of informal advice to the gardeners who happened to be on hand when they were there. The community garden movement in Jamaica Plain grew, and in five years the farm could take credit for some 125 new gardens, both in Jamaica Plain and in bordering communities.

But now it was 1987. The state and its subway were at the farm's front gate. The land immediately to the north was part of the corridor blueprint, and its use still had to be decided. The Station Area Task Force meetings raged on; the factions in favor of housing and those lobbying for greenspace had not budged an inch. But the state couldn't wait another ten years for them to do so.

The farm was well enough recognized as a landscape construction and maintenance operation to enter the discussions. It presented a plan that included basketball courts interspersed with greenspace, sunken playgrounds, and border trees—as well as a request that it be awarded the maintenance contract for what it was calling the Southwest Corridor Park. Impressed, the state agreed.

To loyalists, the farm itself now seemed invincible. But Slug Rosenbaum knew better. Not for nothing had so many local housing advocates fought so hard to stop the highway.

The inevitable day finally arrived. Representatives from one of the community development corporations came forward with a proposal. The time had come, they argued, to return the farmland to the community for much-needed low-income, congregate housing. The farmland had always been designated for housing, and try as they might to ignore it, its members had always known that they were only temporary tenants.

Defenders of the farm shot back: Yes, the farm had started out as a stopgap, but it had taken on a life of its own. It had done every bit as much to engender a sense of connection and community as houses would, maybe more. It had brought a new and invaluable element to community life, a different political dimension—a feisty, hands-on, and deeply primal sense of roots. It had built a neighborhood where none existed and restored a trace of Eden to the most desolate corner of the town.

The conflict reached a painful impasse. The housing advocates held most of the cards, and everyone knew it. But more than houses were at stake here. Friendships and even marriages went on the line. Several gardeners were now married to housing activists who, in more carefree days, had helped them plant their plots. Several members of the farm board quit over the dispute. Others on the board dug in their heels and refused to budge. Neighbors began to avoid one another on the street; kitchen tables fell silent. A deep sadness spread over once-committed and now conflicted soul mates.

It was one of Slug Rosenbaum's finest hours, for which all of his previous turnings had groomed him. He became a liaison between the parties. He established committees from the farm and from the development group and, making no secret of his determination to work out a compromise, saw to it that they met and talked and genuinely listened to one another's views. For more weeks than anyone cared to count, he ferried back and forth between the camps. He attended meetings, lobbied doggedly by phone, listened, and negotiated. Finally, when it seemed as if each side had had their say and could go no further, he produced his plum.

The farm would surrender the orchard. The CDC could develop townhouses on the sacrificed land, on the scheme of the mews that dot chic Beacon Hill. The residents of the new co-ops would have the luxury of surrounding a thriving garden. And the farm—the first positive thing that had sent roots down in this sad place—would stand.

Once, in the inner pages of a book on ferns I'd taken down in an idle hour while visiting friends in the country, I found two small lists. They were written in pencil in a woman's hand in the immediate aftermath of a horrific war, the private catalogue of the ferns and trees she'd identified on her solitary walks.

It is impossible to know, and irresistible not to speculate, whether in these lists of woodland specimens she'd found a sort of faith, and hope, that the world didn't offer elsewhere. Here is what she found, in August 1947: Ferns: interrupted, royal, lady fern, hay scented, marsh, goldie, Christmas, leatherwood, bladder, ostrich, sensitive. And trees: white oak, red maple, sugar maple, shad, tulip, sweet gum, fringe tree, magnolia, poplar, big-toothed aspen, ginkgo, water oak, sycamore, ash, ash-leaved maple, redbud.

It is never a bad place to begin: naming the green things, and loving them. I thought this at the time, and I think it now whenever I pass by the farm. The generation of progressives, old Catholics, Latinos, and upwardly mobile African-Americans who inherited a despoiled garden turned to one another to achieve what earlier generations had pursued in more private ways along the rows of wire fence and pickets—not, perhaps, from any higher moral ground of collectivism but because the times had changed. When Winky Cloherty freely rambled the streets and hopped the trains, when streets were community institutions in the best sense of the word, proper gardens were as natural as clover, a generosity not just of means but of spirit. But to pull off such a thing in 1976, kindred souls had needed to carefully husband the spark of vision: that where you envision possibility, you harvest abundance.

Come August, the corn will be high, and the coreopsis will tower above the tops of the chain link. Basil and tomatoes will peek out over billowy banks of sage. Squash and morning glories will entwine in full bloom. Neighbors will gather for yet another workday, pruning and straightening the common beds around the perimeter, cleaning the paths, and refurbishing the compost bin.

This year there will be more new faces than usual. A few of the older members have grown too infirm to do the work, the volunteer coordinator named Jennifer tells me. The community "lost" one of their number over the winter. Another has moved away. But Jennifer still has a waiting list of about ten. And on hot summer evenings, while the adult residents of the low-income co-ops next door pull a card table out on the sidewalk for a game of pinochle, or sit with their grandchildren in open doorways, two youngsters leap as high as they can to pluck some apricots from a laden tree, pick the raspberries that poke through the mesh fence, and gather a few pansies that wash the concrete perimeter in deep shades of purple, the color of suffering and kings.

And as for Slug, one day in the midst of the struggle he found himself pacing the streets in turmoil. A week earlier he had been informed that as a ranking city employee, he would have to campaign for his "boss" in the midst of a hotly contested mayoral race, producing a quota of petition signatures each month. He'd walked out of his office and hadn't been back since. Every milestone in his own political journey now came back to him. He saw the broad swath of territory he'd traversed, from the radical undergraduate he'd been, to the community reformer he'd become. He stood at a crossroads. And as he wrestled with how to respond to this unacceptable demand on him, how to keep body and soul together, an unexpected thought crossed his mind: "I probably should have been a farmer."

At first it was startling. But as he walked along, it began to sink in, and as he talked and wrote around the dining room on Clive Street, it sat surprisingly comfortably. The next day he resigned. He bought a used truck and gathered the tools in his garage. He put out word that he was available for landscaping services, under a name that said more than any explanation ever could: Down to Earth.

BUILDING

---·-·-·-·-·-·-·-·---

The mixed nature of the neighborhood keeps you honest. Life is simpler here and the values are very basic ones.

—JOHN MESSERVY, *a resident*

MY NEXT-DOOR NEIGHBOR NANCY, an honorable old Yankee with a passion for the Red Sox, was born in the house she still lives in. She can rattle off the genealogy of every back door from hers all the way to the main road and up the other side, then out in a number of other directions—doorways that flung open, and lives that entwined her own and those of her three children, until the latter moved away, to return from time to time to share a meal, watch a ball game, and help clean her birdbath.

In recent years the average stay at our end of the street has been about twenty years, four times that of the average American family anywhere. This is good for houses, and it is good for neighborhoods. The first time I stepped through my front door, there was something—call it history or devas or love. The rooms were full of it, as any number of grander places hadn't been. We felt oddly claimed, the way one does in abbeys and barns. The ghosts of what had taken root and lived here seemed to thrive on, in spite of human intentions, in the breathing crevices.

We settled in. We sanded and scrubbed and, like diligent novices, absorbed the stories of the house that had let us in. Pennies had been hoarded here, that was clear; awful mustard walls endured; plywood was used for kitchen cupboards. A generation back, a grand piano stood where our upright does now, and every night, we learned, a father fingered lullabies to his as-yet-unborn child. In time the splendid three-trunked ash out back became that child's magic grove. Old fieldstones were dragged in to mend a crumbling wall. We found the stones of the place as lovely as its tales.

We basked in their shelter as we set about cutting out new flower beds, making our own rhythms, arranging furniture. We came to honor them as progenitors of the place, their emblems our own starting point, as if they *were* our own—never realizing that, in time, they were becoming so.

And besides the stones: the old wooden towel rack fixed to the window frame in the kitchen; who would have thought to append something at precisely the eye level of the average man? But we wouldn't for a fortune consider moving it. Or the rusted horseshoe nailed into the clapboards at the northeast corner. Who put it there? And with what prayer or dream?

In our turn we became characters in the much more elaborate story of our street. There was the notorious dinner party of 1989, at which Wagner Lesser defended Pol Pot to the death. And the Christmas "do" where, among the blue jeans and long festive skirts, the shrimp and carrot sticks, the long-single Steve announced his engagement to happy tears. And the star that went out in our sky forever the day we learned of

Chris's death in Wisconsin's waters. The christenings, the wakes, the back-yard barbecues. The Christmas jams, cups of sugar and tea . . . bringing an infant home and having the whole block rush out to welcome him. Once, when I inadvertently locked the door on an egg frying on the stove, it was Chick next door who saved the day, smashing my back window while Nancy kept the baby happy, plying him with lemon cookies.

A home, no matter how tight a sanctuary, is never a wholly private affair. It is the threshold across which our common chronicle passes, coming in and going out like a tide that gathers us, denizens of a particular place, into a creation that is unique in all the world.

For most of us, it is among neighbors more than family these days that we come by life's great occasions for generosity, sympathy, and tolerance—even, if we are very lucky, affection. Nancy reads the *Herald*, I read the *Globe*; but both of us love Mozart, and three-part harmony to our Christmas carols. The Connaughton sisters across the street resolutely opposed the speed bump that I argued would moderate our high-voltage traffic, but they have given me voluptuous cuttings of oxalis and impatiens to warm my winter sills. Though we differ even as to the politics of neighborhood life, we make room for one another, for our quirks, perspectives, for compromise. The more time we spend together, the easier it becomes, the richer our story, and paradoxically, with frisky little cairns and old ladies in green Cadillacs, the more authentic, too.

We all know that there is another way to live in cities. We imagine it as sequences of black-and-white shorts from a country we will never visit. To live behind triple dead bolts and spy holes in a place where everyone you pass has no name, where every vestibule and footfall is suspect, where our routes and habits—the way we walk to the grocery store, the hours we come in and go out, even the way we answer our phones—are covert and, by design, self-extinguishing. This we cannot imagine enduring, but I know from firsthand experience that it happens.

At some point my grandmother's respectable working-class neighborhood of two- and three-bedroom homes in Buffalo, New York, "turned." Her German and Italian and Irish neighbors sold to shiftless nonfamilies, single people with babies by a variety of men who came and went in loud cars, or stayed and partied, fought and broke windows. Gardens, once burgeoning with prize roses and peonies, fell to ruin. Paint jobs were neglected, social service workers seemed as regular as the postman. Still, my grandmother hung on. Each morning she set out with sad, proud defiance to the dying plaza where she bought her groceries, praying she wouldn't be mugged. Widowed and caring for a disabled daughter, she couldn't bring herself to part with her few remaining friends of fifty years, with her memories, with her life.

Only once did she leave her beloved neighborhood: to visit her sister for a week in Florida. In her absence her home was ransacked. Furniture was soiled, clothing yanked out of every drawer, the jewelry box overturned. The kitchen was the worst: a lifetime of Green Stamp china in shambles on the spotless linoleum. But as there was nothing of any material worth among her possessions, nothing was taken—if you exclude dignity, a sense of coherence, peace of mind.

It happens that people live this way. And while my way of life speaks of something vital, and my grandmother's of something dying, they have this in common: my grandmother knew what I am learning, that one's neighbors are not simply part of the landscape or "opportunities" for friendship—they are life itself. Now that I too live on such terms with a place, I understand why people endure what my grandmother did. She left, four years after the break-in, only out of fear for her daughter and with a broken heart.

Isn't this community? Haven't I found what I came here for and settled in search of? Tolerance, generosity, cooperation, lives sufficiently connected at a deeper reality than the surface flotsam of politesse? A place where we lend ourselves to moments of celebration and grief alike—even, to some degree, to a sense of shared fate?

By almost any public philosophy of community, the answer would be: yes. And: not quite.

Whether we call ourselves the street life of our neighborhood, or participants in the common language of shared habits and values, or simply the human web that supports informal ways of helping, our communally owned lawn mowers and swapped house keys and fall garden harvests are the humus of community in the same way that my horseshoe, my stone walls, and my quirky water meter are the foundations of my home.

Even more (and from the viewpoint of community, this is key): these regular patterns seem to enable all of us to get on with the higher order of our business as human beings, our vocations and work, in ways that unpredictability and disruption thwart. Freed of the need to continually remake and defend our nests, we are more able to proceed with the work of contributing to the culture.

But the test of real community is something else: the extent to which it copes with challenges to its continuation and protects the existing lives that feed and are fed by it. Rootedness goes a long way in preserving community. It may even be essential. But it can't, alone, defend a place against direct threat, whether physical or ideological.

To hear old-timers tell it, Jamaica Plain was once a honeycomb of neighborhoods like mine. Each had its own identity and lore, but they shared a remarkably healthy street life and cohesiveness. As the town grew from a collection of farms and pretty suburban estates into a residential pocket in an expanding city in the mid-1800s, it acquired factory operatives as well as downtown professionals, roofers, masons, painters, and carpenters. Soon J.P. offered something for nearly every pocketbook. Suburbanlike homes with sizable yards were set cheek by jowl with brick townhouses. Queen Anne–style homes overlooked wood-frame double- and triple-deckers, and these, the row houses of the blue-collar sections.

My neighborhood, Moss Hill, is one of the stablest in J.P. A series of subdivided estates, it holds single-family homes on quarter-acre lots. We arrange our privacy by way of hedges and shades. Considered J.P.'s "high rent" district, the prices here have consistently outpaced those of similar homes closer to Centre Street. But not by much. Thus it is a desirable prospect for prospering black and Hispanic professionals, racially mixed couples, and gays who are looking for a retreat into semi-suburban calm at day's end without completely relinquishing the tempo of city life. Diverse, integrated, and tolerant, it is a rare professional enclave by any standards, and increasingly its residents come and stay precisely for these qualities.

To get to "downtown" J.P., I take the footpath across the street up through the backside of wooded lots, then turn down Moss Hill, with its comfortable homes and stunning views of downtown shining in the haze of morning sun. I quickly pass along the pond, then cut through a neighborhood of grand Victorians in Pondside. These are divided now into spacious condos, and here too the streets are relatively quiet at midday. Professional as well, the residents are more likely to be teachers, newspaper reporters, and social workers than doctors and lawyers as in Moss Hill. Next, moving north toward downtown, I traverse a street where friends with two children live in the upstairs of a two-family home that they own and finance by renting the first floor.

This housing diversity and the resulting mix of residents make J.P. unique among Boston neighborhoods. Each sub-neighborhood has a feeling of completeness about it. Within each one, children, families, and older retirees provide the makings for a rich street life through the course of the day. People are out and about at all hours, walking babies or dogs, returning from Centre Street, riding bikes, watching one another's children. There are places for students and for first-time home buyers ready to begin families or settle near cousins, brothers, or grandparents. Most important, people here traditionally could—and did (and can, and still do)—move up, or down, the economic scale without being forced to leave the community as their incomes and leisure interests changed. And they find in the tonier neighborhoods many of the same characteristics of the old ones. It isn't at all uncommon here to have lived at several addresses before settling down into a final home, yet never once leave Jamaica Plain's three-square-mile limits.

In two more short blocks, I come to the residential district past Hyde Square. Named for its commercial center, it is really a network of streets on which double- and triple-deckers hold recent immigrant families between the shops of Centre Street and the Southwest Corridor. Hyde Square today is home to the Hispanic community in Jamaica Plain, the largest Spanish-speaking community in New England. It is comprised of Puerto Ricans, Hondurans, Guatemalans, Cubans, and Dominicans, as well as a smattering of Cambodians, West Indians, and working-class whites.

By nearly every measure, Hyde Square is Moss Hill's counterpart. Where Moss Hill has evolved gradually over the past twenty-five years, its social changes moderated by the dynamics of private home ownership, Hyde Square has been torn apart, deconstructed by disinvestment into a no-man's-land much like my grandmother's on the faded north side of Buffalo, New York, twenty years ago.

Had Hyde Square disintegrated completely, it is hard to imagine what Jamaica Plain would be like today. Not only would our interlinking of class and race, rich and poor, the disenfranchised and the empowered, have utterly broken down, as it has in too many other places, but so too would any legitimate claims to our being a community in any meaningful sense of the word. If its story had died, our collective story would have died with it. We would no longer be the place we claim to be and are proud of being, a place of accommodation, hope, and possibility. That it didn't is a story that deserves telling.

Karen Chacon is thirty-two years old. She lives in an attractive two-bedroom townhouse in Hyde Square that she has owned since 1994. Today she is satisfied that she has managed to provide her two daughters, whose portraits dot the bookcases in her modest living room, with a sense of continuity and connection. But it has taken years of struggle. Warm but exact, with pale blue eyes and a no-nonsense mien, Karen is the sort of woman who expects accounts to be kept right, the floor swept, the details of the house in line. She has learned to respect the unifying orders.

Karen was two when her family moved into a two-bedroom working-class house on Edge Hill Street just outside Hyde Square. The year was 1966, and though the actual geography that the family had traversed (in typical J.P. fashion) was slight—a mere seven blocks from the industrial Brookside neighborhood to the south—in psychological terms it was enormous. With their arrival on Edge Hill, her parents had achieved the long-dreamed-of status of home owners. Now they could become long-term citizens of their world—raise their children, see them off into the world, and grow old with a bevy of grandchildren drifting back onto the familiar streets for regular visits.

As we set out for a walk around the old streets, Karen vividly recalls these days for me. We pass homes all nearly alike and set close, like a brood of contented hens sheltering us from the bustle of traffic on nearby Centre Street.

"It was great. The whole street was large families," Karen says. "All my friends that I hung out with and went to school with all had big families. When we first moved in, it was all Irish."

Inside the house was a world peopled by countless aunts, uncles, cousins. And out the front door was everyone's back yard. Families relied on one another. When anything happened, someone was there to help, there with food, there to care for the kids.

On a rise behind us sprawls the concrete edifice of the Hennigan Middle School. Beyond it towers a conglomerate of brick buildings and exhaust flues, industrial chimneys that, while I know they are the remains of a former high school, the veterans' hospital, and factories, have a chilling effect: as if to say that the halcyon spell of these tiny streets in their shadow is a chimera, its children bound for disillusionment. I look away.

Four blocks away in the opposite direction rises the looming bulk of the Bromley-Heath projects, a city-within-a-city of low- and high-rise apartments where most of J.P.'s African-American population resides. Bromley was built in 1954. In time it would become one of the first tenant-owned and -managed projects in the country, with its own radio station and newspaper, health center and credit union. But at the time it was just another ghetto project with all the underclass problems such developments contain. Between the middle school and Bromley sat the small valley of Karen's world.

"For a long time, *that* was 'Bromley' and *this* was 'J.P.,'"
she tells me. "Walden Street was the boundary line. You didn't
cross that line, and there was no connection."

In the child's view of the world, the tense interchange of
race relations came together not in the abstractions of fear or
media reports but on the playground.

"We used to play at the playground at the Hennigan
School"—she nods in its direction—"me and my little sister.
And we used to get jumped every day by this group of girls
who came up from Bromley.

"They'd push us around and intimidate us. We'd run home
crying, every day. Or we'd see them coming, and we'd take off.
It was a really hard time. But that was how I met my friend
from Honduras. She lived on the hill above the park, and she
used to watch us, every day, getting pushed around by this
group of girls. One time she came down and yelled at the kids
and defended us. And we didn't get beat up. Then she looked
at us and she said, 'I've been watching you for a week, getting
your butt kicked every day. The next time I see them pushing
you around, *I'm* going to beat you up!'"

Karen laughs. "So we became really good friends. The three
of us would go down to the park together and say, 'You want
to pick a fight? Come on!' And of course, it stopped."

After that, friendships came peacefully to the environs of
Edge Hill. The first Hispanic family to move into the neighborhood were Puerto Rican. They lived off Day Street. Then
another family, the Sanchezes, moved onto Edge Hill, bringing
with them a handful of playmates for Karen. The older Karen
got, the more international the composition of her group became. There was a girl from Trinidad, her childhood friend

from Honduras, and another from Puerto Rico. Karen was the token white girl. Her best friend was African-American.

This is how neighborhoods look to us who live in them, whether we're middle-class or poor or somewhere in between. It is the relationships that form, the ebb and flow of life unfolding. Through the seventies, as the skin tones of the children on those streets grew more varied, nothing significant happened to threaten families' expectations of their futures there. Each day Karen walked to Blessed Sacrament School three blocks away, and when it let out, she hung with her friends at Rizzo's Pizza or at the bowling lanes in Hyde Square.

"Our friends were always mixed races. My older brothers and sisters were teenagers. And all their friends had their cars jacked up in the back, you know, with their rear ends really high? They had loud mufflers, and they'd do drag races up and down the street. There was a lot of pot smoking and that sort of stuff. But there was a lot of fun stuff, too. Back then it was bowling, sports, the library, Girl Scouts."

Then suddenly it seemed as if the tide of common life had run amok, was pulling to a foreign moon. One day the family across the street was gone. And then another. One building had a new owner; and in less than a year, another one—this time a bank or the city. Pockets of seediness, "bad sorts," appeared. Properties went neglected. No one was quite sure who to blame. Around the corner a vacant house was set on fire. A drug bust netted a cache of crack cocaine.

In this, the lives of neighborhoods are vastly different from our stories about them. They are complicated enough that ruptures, when they occur, come at us as if from out of the blue. Arbitrary, the changes seem, and incremental, with no real turning points, no embodied villains, and no respect whatsoever for rationally unfolding narrative.

In the distant background was the Southwest Corridor. Well back on the other side of Centre Street, it had hemorrhaged houses and families. On the streets that ran through Karen's neighborhood, the misery was confined to abandonment and negligent landlords. Perhaps the demise of the highway project had cast doubt on the continued viability of the neighborhoods on its periphery. Perhaps older home owners and landlords didn't want to deal with the new tides of ethnic immigrants coming in, or the drug culture that was driving its grim white lines deeper into the heart of Hyde Square. They failed to maintain their properties; they fell into arrears; they gave up.

It began at the fringes, along the streets that bordered the projects. Walden Street was the worst, to hear Karen tell it, a den of terror: drugs, muggings, and casual violence. But then it started to edge into Hyde Square. Into the rubble-strewn lots crept pushers and their customers. No longer were these customers well-heeled yuppies who could speed down Tremont Street and pause for a hit on one of the main intersections. They were kids from the neighborhood who could afford the cheap crack that was breaking on the scene.

The fabric was disintegrating; the sense of continuity, of relationship, the tendrils of home, and the unspoken compacts people made with one another were withering. The work of genuine *dwelling*—of building neighbors, fostering friendships on the street and with merchants—was replaced by a vacuum where anything that could happen did happen.

Conversation devolved into the swapping of horror stories, tolerance to barely suppressed bigotry. What group was responsible for bringing what "stuff" in? The home owners became "us," the projects "them."

Throw into the mix her family's demise, her parents' divorce, and being so harassed as a Catholic schoolgirl in a tough public high school that it was easier to drop out, and the forces around which Karen—or my grandmother, or anyone else for that matter—could declare common cause with others seemed so massive and multiple as to defy correction. Absentee landlords, speculators, crime, drugs. The personal isolation into which one creeps is like a startling, almost beguiling trap.

"I was seeing my boyfriend, and I was seeing school," says Karen. "That was it. It was just him and me in our little world. We hung out at Rizzo's, and we'd go to Jamaica Pond."

At sixteen she married a Salvadoran, changed her name to Chacon, and fled to a corner of town where the seams still held.

Midway down Centre between Hyde Square and Walden Street loomed the imposing hulk of Blessed Sacrament Church. As recently as 1970, three thousand parishioners had attended the memorial Mass for the late Cardinal Cushing there. Blueprints had been drawn up to expand the high school.

But by the mid-eighties, it was a stretch to count even eight hundred on the rolls. The high school was closed. The grammar school population had dwindled from 650 to 230. Blessed Sacrament had long since been declared a "mission church" by the archdiocese, which meant that what it took in on Sundays didn't come close to maintaining its upkeep.

But numbers alone don't adequately depict the strength of a mission church. The three priests and several remaining nuns at Blessed Sacrament had redirected their mission to the acute needs of the neighborhood. Spanish was now spoken in the rectory as often as English by these mainly Irish-American clergy, and they relished using the political savvy that had served earlier generations of priests in working the system on behalf of their immigrant flocks. The Holy Name Society had given way to an arson task force, a food pantry, and efforts to find homes for those displaced by fires and spotty gentrification. On Good Friday now, rather than kneel in the traditional ritual of penitence for several hours in the nave of the darkened church, parishioners staged a "Stations of the Cross" march through the neighborhood, stopping at drug shooting galleries and burned-out buildings where they prayed aloud for the people inside and for city officials to come to their aid.

But the island of safety that Blessed Sacrament represented seemed to shrink daily. And as time went by, the old people, who no longer opened their doors to strangers, grew reluctant even to come out to pray.

The people of Blessed Sacrament knew that good works alone couldn't reverse the forces decimating the neighborhood. But there was no local government to appeal to, and the city bureaucracy was too overwhelmed and remote. Besides: to whom would they have appealed? The police seemed powerless to stop the drugs. The fire department was always one step behind the burnings. And there is no general public responsibility for the oversight of disinvestment in the private housing market, no commissioner of community life. The public role in housing at the time (to name just one of the community's most obvious problems) was a hodgepodge of federal and state jurisdictions that generally came into play only when an area had so decayed that its remaining structures had to be razed and new congregate housing, like Bromley-Heath, erected in its place, administered like small dependent colonies from offices many miles away.

A number of citizens on the other side of Centre Street, people like Sue Naimark, John Rouse, and others, had tried to create ways to keep the remaining houses in their area safe, occupied, and intact. John and Sue were part of a group that rehabbed vacant triple-deckers with city funds and sold them, with the stipulation that the new owners had to live in the buildings for at least one year. The program had limited success, but it did pave the way for a local role in housing development on that side of town. When the Station Area Task Force group decided to build affordable housing along the Southwest Corridor, it was to some of these activists that they turned to do the work.

But such thinking hadn't crossed Centre Street, because no one thought of Hyde Square as having open, developable land, and because no mechanisms existed in the affordable redevelopment world for single-structure projects that would preserve the integrity of a neighborhood's existing housing character.

But the political winds would soon shift in a direction favorable to the people of Blessed Sacrament. In 1983 Ray Flynn was elected mayor of Boston by a progressive coalition of city-wide neighborhood activists. "The mayor of the neighborhoods," Flynn vowed to make the residential quality of life a priority. One of his first acts was to establish neighborhood councils. The councils were to be local bodies with broad-based advisory powers on everything from neighborhood zoning, safety, and development issues to parks, public services, and human services. The residents of Hyde Square soon had a recognizable group of local residents to appeal to who could convey their concerns to city hall.

Flynn did something else. As a nod for their campaign support, he embraced local nonprofit housing development corporations. A census of vacant city-owned lots was undertaken and netted 747 that were considered buildable. Soon monies were being channeled into locally run redevelopment projects on many of these sites. Four of them were in Hyde Square. In 1989 the Jamaica Plain Neighborhood Development Corporation was awarded the contract to develop them.

The question was: what to do with them? The practice of housing redevelopment still hadn't evolved a solution for single-structure projects. And these were just that, single and scattered.

As members of the Neighborhood Development Corporation drove around the Hyde Square neighborhood exploring the terrain in search of answers, they made a startling discovery. Many more vacant lots existed than anyone had realized. Most hadn't shown up in the city census—to be exact, twenty-six. And this number didn't count the lots on which dilapidated, abandoned, and arson-threatened structures still stood. These twenty-six lots didn't fall under any proposed city rehab plan; they simply sat idle.

A local woman named Betsaida Gutierrez was in a unique position to understand what all of this could mean. She'd lived in Hyde Square for years. She kept a garden at the community farm and had been a longtime member of Jamaica Plain's tenants' rights group, City Life. Betsaida had seen the community change, and she'd seen the efforts of residents to save it. As it happened, she also worked at the Jamaica Plain Neighborhood Development Corporation.

Now Betsaida persuaded her colleagues that they couldn't simply proceed with business as usual. The neighborhood needed more than four—or even twenty-six—new homes. It needed trust and restored tolerance, moral and psychological reinvestment every bit as much as it needed new doors and locks.

Before the Neighborhood Development Corporation lay not just a development opportunity, Betsaida argued, but an empowerment project that could turn the routine formula of inner-city revitalization on its ear. Betsaida proposed that, instead of coming up with a plan of their own and merely seeking the community's approval, they knock on people's doors and get residents involved in the design of those lost acres; neighbors could approach the city with their own plan—and in the process begin to meet one another face-to-face again.

This, in essence, is what happened. The NDC approached the neighborhood council with a version of Betsaida's plan. Before embarking on any initiative that might result in the development of all twenty-six city-owned lots, they wanted to convey to city hall a tentative sense of grassroots support. Second, they wanted to draw in the rest of Jamaica Plain and restitch frayed community connections through council representatives. Third, the NDC hoped to elicit the help of City Life in the early stages of door knocking. The tenants' rights group had recently swept the neighborhood council seats and had strong ties in Hyde Square. Their lists and their street outreach workers would be invaluable. The neighborhood council unanimously approved Betsaida's vision, and soon the door knocking began.

It was slow, painstaking work. Just getting people to release their safety latches took several visits. Things were bad—what else was new? Everyone in the neighborhood was well aware that the priests at Blessed Sacrament had recently managed to bring city leaders in for a high-level discussion about drug and crime and garbage. The mayor, the police commissioner, and a number of other officials had all attended. The meeting had just gotten under way when it was sabotaged by a firebombing directly across the street. Thereafter SWAT teams moved into an apartment in the square. New arson signs went up on graffitied firetraps. But no one was optimistic. If the authorities couldn't change much, how could *they* hope to do any better? Most just wanted out.

One of those who knocked on doors during this period recalls the despair she discovered cowering behind them.

"I remember it vividly. People were really discouraged," she says. "A lot of them wanted to move. They were really afraid of the vacant lots, and the crime. People just kept on saying, 'We've got to get out of here. It's really bad.' And the lots *were* bad," she says. "There were hypodermic needles, nasty stuff. A chop shop. For real, it was bad. People wanted to get out."

If it had been a less desperate time, the more conservative old-timers on Edge Hill, Roundhill, and Day Streets would probably have closed their doors on these young people with their newfangled notions of what they called community-controlled housing. But with little to show for their crime watches and anti-arson groups, they agreed with the door knockers on at least one point: they weren't ready to surrender their neighborhood yet, not to anyone.

On July 26, 1990, some one hundred of them showed up in the basement of Blessed Sacrament and began to share their stories. People like Bill Allan told of a place that had vanished. In 1979 he'd moved into Hyde Square to run a home for retarded adults. Several years later the state changed its funding guidelines, and he thought he would have to close down. But the local neighborhood association bought the building and paid him to manage it, it was so unthinkable that the home would move. People told stories of limbo, of efforts to make it in America, to raise and educate decent children only to have them caught up in drugs and crime.

Most of those present had never met before; some had seen one another in passing and looked away quickly, the way one did those days. Stories filled the room that night, stories of strangers who shared only the fact that they were there and wanted a place to call home, with all that that implied. From the hesitant and cautionary voices of the past to the younger, bewildered voices of disappointed hope, it gradually became clear that their numbers were larger than just a tiny band of hangers-on, and their words the beginning of a new story, one they were telling together. With the combined skills, talents, and savvy in the room that night, they might actually make a difference.

The group met again a month later. They were public hous-

ing tenants, home owners, parents of young children, single
mothers and grandparents, priests and nuns, political refugees
and humble sanitation workers. They argued back and forth, in
Spanish and English, about what to do, what they wanted, and
how to go about it. A few wanted to turn the vacant lots into
gardens like the community farm, but others argued that the
best way to rebuild the neighborhood would be to give people
homes. Everyone eventually agreed. The question was: how
many homes, and what kind, and how to proceed?

Betsaida and her boss, Ricanne Hadrian, began to lay out
the arcana of real estate development for the residents of Hyde
Square—finance options, issues of site disposition and design.
And with these in hand, community members evolved a plan.
They would build forty-one new homes, to be offered at mixed
income rates to Jamaica Plain home buyers in the form of a
relatively unknown entity: scattered site equity co-ops.

The co-ops seemed to have all the stabilizing benefits of
home ownership while at the same time protecting properties
from a profit structure that had led to some of the neighborhood's worst problems. Their financing was a joint arrangement
of funding "syndicates" (usually banks, foundations, and public
finance in exchange for tax credits) and home owners. Owners
buy shares of their units, with a cap placed on the amount of
inflation allowed to accrue to them as profit should they sell
them. In this way, limited-equity co-ops allow for a considerable income mix among residents. In the case of those in Hyde
Square, half would be sold to people earning 50 percent of
Boston's median income, with the rest balanced above and below this median.

Traditionally, limited-equity co-ops have been multiple-dwelling units. The innovation that Hyde Square residents came up with was to employ the limited-equity concept, bundled for financing and management purposes, but preserve the neighborhood's single-structure housing stock and way of life.

The plans were as impressive as the process had been. The city, eager to see the lots well used, agreed to issue an RFP (Request for Proposals) in line with the residents' plan, virtually ensuring that they, with the logistical and technical help of the Neighborhood Development Corporation, would be the developers.

Now it was up to them to make it a reality. Over the next six months, residents learned about site control, the complicated red tape of regulatory approval, how to issue and evaluate bids, and finally how to fill the homes (or "rent up") once they were finished.

In the course of debating issues like whether to create common or private outdoor space and whether to dedicate assigned parking spots, neighbors confronted thorny issues of lifestyle and ethnic preferences, responsibility, courtesy, security, and trust—issues that in the past had been simply a part of the ambient tide, fortified by earlier generations. In creating new homes, they found themselves addressing the norms of the community that would arise in their midst. Working fathers who'd never had the chance or the time found themselves voicing dreams for playgrounds; single mothers for reciprocal help with children on the street. Images of the old Hyde Square came to life in the confines of the Blessed Sacrament meetings as housewives, teachers, and fathers articulated their hopes for its future.

If they learned more about housing and community development than they ever expected to know, residents also learned a lot more about one another and about the multifaceted nature of making a home. The importance of forming alliances and effective partnerships couldn't be exaggerated—not just between one another but with larger Jamaica Plain and the city. For the neighborhood to survive and prevail against the forces that had nearly torn it apart, residents needed to form effective relationships at every level of the larger community and within decision-making structures: with city hall, with law enforcement, with the banks, and with counterpart organizations in Jamaica Plain and across the city.

Street by street, neighborhood associations started to form again in Hyde Square. Crime watches were revitalized. At neighborhood council meetings, regular reports were made on the progress of the Hyde Square co-op initiative. At the city level years of networking were paying off. Former allies were now in decision-making roles in city hall, and the NDC was in close contact with them. Peers in other neighborhoods and statewide consortia gave advice. On one "work day" Hyde Square residents were able to visit co-ops elsewhere in the city, giving them the benefit of a broader view and raising the profile and legitimacy of their own project. The isolation that had ravaged them and their neighborhood was breaking down. New bonds were being formed, not just for the project but for the future leaders within the community.

In many ways the most important bonds to be reestablished were with the more influential constituencies in Jamaica Plain. The fate of that neighborhood mattered. It wasn't some distant abstraction, it was just around the corner. Its crime and destitution affected everyone. Ricanne Hadrian, Betsaida's boss at the NDC, was tireless in communicating with the elected state and local representatives who lived among the opinion makers and professionals on Moss Hill and elsewhere in town. Hyde Square was on the way back, and their support, tacit or explicit, official or circumstantial, was important.

On April 28, 1992, neighbors gathered for the ground breaking of the first co-op in Hyde Square. To those close to the project, it felt as if a new generation of children were being welcomed to the old sod—unknown, untested, full of promise. And with the poetic justice that only local weavers of tales can achieve, they would appear precisely where hope was most desperately needed, on Walden Street.

Karen moved back to Hyde Square in 1993. Recently separated and with two daughters to support, she moved in with her mother and spent many of her days walking in the neighborhood, sizing up the changes since she'd left, trying to work out the pieces of a new life. One day she saw a notice for an available apartment on Walden Street. With a certain trepidation she went to see it. It was one of the new co-ops. It was clean and up-to-date, and it suited her needs. She was back in the neighborhood.

In the days and weeks that followed, she found that, even though the faces had changed, life out on the streets was oddly familiar. It was a different story from the one of her childhood, yet in many ways the same. More than new walls had gone up. A new consciousness of community had emerged. People were more aware of what was happening. They were more likely to talk to their neighbors. Did you see that guy trying to break into that car last night? Fifteen or twenty years ago there hadn't been crime watches. They hadn't had neighborhood associations or phone trees.

The parks had been brought back. There were more children on the streets again, youngsters with their mothers, and the older set, working out turf issues back at the old playground. More Latino families were becoming home owners, and more were taking leadership positions on the neighborhood council and in the merchants' associations.

We've stopped for coffee at the Black Crow Caffe around the corner from Karen's place, and this woman who just a few years ago had checked out of the scene tells me how grateful and proud she is of what's happened here. Her children see their grandmother and aunt almost daily after school. Often they stay for dinner when Karen works late, playing in the streets with the residents who've moved in since they were born. Karen has taken a job as a community organizer and works in several new NDC projects around town.

She tells me, "I remember getting flyers in my door, for community meetings. I never read them. I'd open them. 'What is it going to do for me right now? Is it going to pay my rent? Is it going to help me pay that light bill that's about to be shut off in two days?' And if it couldn't?" She shrugs. "They'd go right in the trash. What the hell did I want a meeting for?

"Now I know. You've got to have those people out there knocking on your door. You've got to have the flyer dropped off. It's funny. I don't know how, back then, I couldn't find the time to go to a community meeting, when I do so much now."

To a certain extent, we learn how to live in a house only after we have one. Moving in, experiencing ownership, I discovered new responsibilities of both a practical and a moral nature. The place where we eat and sleep is also the composite of our lives, past and future, where what we cherish is stored and cared for and shared. It is sacred ground in this sense, the center from which each day we move out into the world and bring the world back in: as workers, lovers, friends, and parents. The impulse to care and to preserve our home gives rise to the patterns and the internal order that make it distinctly ours. More than anything else, I've learned that a home is built by repetitions.

Around such repetitions much of life is fulfilled. Structures build upon structures, and before long, if conditions are right, the habits of home reach their arms into the larger tide of any neighborhood worthy of the name.

"I see people coming back, and I see people staying," Karen tells me. "I see a lot of people who I haven't seen in years. If they're not living here, they're working here. This guy I used to know when I was a kid. He grew up on Runnells Street. I used to have a crush on him. I ran into him and I said, 'What the hell are you doing back here?' And he said, 'I'm working in this organization helping people with addiction problems. They get sober and I help them find a job and housing.'

"And I said, 'Isn't it funny? You moved away too, but now you're back.' And he said, 'Yeah. And I love it.'"

BUYING AND SELLING

The commercial districts are the livings rooms of Jamaica Plain.
— "A Plan for Jamaica Plain," 1985

FOR A LONG TIME IN JAMAICA PLAIN people were happy
with hamburger. There was Doyle's, and it stood by itself on
the periphery like a staunch watering hole in the wilderness.
Years went by, and there were mumblings from time to time,
but everyone knew what they'd bargained for in moving to a
place where Zagat's never ventured.

And then, one day, it happened. (And there were mumblings
about this, too, but really who could argue with the fundamental premise of it all, its populism, its undisputed elegance as a
multicultural cuisine, or—least of all—what it said about the
long and steady rehabilitation of our Centre Street.)

Jamaica Plain said *yes* to gourmet pizza.

One Friday night, shortly after an obligatory evening of ho-
mage to hamburger, I make my way to the opposite end of
town, and into another, newer scene. A hip group of black
women in caftans and braids occupies the window spot beneath
the gold-foil moon and orders Pellegrinos. Grilled chicken Cae-

sars waft by. By the time my pizza has been delivered to my hand-painted blue-and-yellow flea-market table, the place is filling up. Behind the counter, owner Kathie Mainzer, whose hair this winter is blond, stuffs a few bills into the register and comes to sit for a minute.

Kathie goes way back in the neighborhood. One day, at the age of twenty-two she woke up, left a bad scene, and found herself with no place to go and an infant daughter to care for. With the moxie that would come to be her trademark, she talked her way into a job as spokeswoman for the Massachusetts Coalition for the Homeless, and for six years she inveighed at state and city officials to fund programs for poor women who had fallen out of the web of community.

By then, her young daughter was setting off to school every day down the streets of Hyde Square. Shootings and drug deals were becoming commonplace. From distant Beacon Hill, where she was hobnobbing with lawmakers, it rankled her. And the day a fourteen-year-old boy was shot on the Hernandez school playground she finally said, enough. She quit her job and organized a coalition of neighborhood groups. Citizens for Safety worked aggressively with state and local law officials to stanch the flow of guns into the neighborhood. They negotiated a citywide gun buyback, ran sports programs for gangs, and facilitated numerous gang mediations in the Hyde and Egleston Square neighborhoods. Largely through their efforts, the streets grew quieter and safer again.

As she relaxes tonight during the happy hour lull, Kathie could be talking about any one of these topics. Or she could be talking anchovies. After years of rallies, marches, and speeches, she has become an entrepreneur. Her gourmet pizza business, Bella Luna, draws the entire spectrum of J.P.'s urban mosaic out into the main drag of Hyde Square. Tonight is typical. The tables are filling with Hispanic and Caribbean patrons, black professionals and white couples, and young women like Kathie once was herself, a two-step away from the shocks of single parenthood. This, Kathie reasoned when she first envisioned the place, is one of the great beauties of pizza. It is also one of the great beauties of small business.

Across the street the Santa Niño de Atocha has been closed for the evening, its grates securely drawn. A storefront botanica, the Santa Niño features the ritual props favored by local practitioners of the voodoo-Christian crossbreed Santeria. Candles, oils, and saints are housed in glass pharmacy cases facing the door. Nearby is a shrine to what looks like the Infant of Prague bedecked in a strand of blue votary beads before a lighted votive and a giant gumball machine. Patrons come here not only for the tools of their oblations but for spiritual consultations as well.

The Santa Niño has been around for as long as anyone can remember, and as I dip into my mezzaluna salad (goat cheese, mesclun, black olives), I am glad that I live in a place where our commerce satisfies both our physical wants and our spiritual needs. At its best, this is what good economic behavior is all about.

Goods drift in and out of our lives, some at a giddy speed, others at leisure, and to a certain extent the life cycle of our attachment to them is determined by how and where and from whom they were acquired. The same can be said for what today we call services, that glut of advice, prepared meals, and remedies that fill up our hours. In what way are we humanized by our buying behaviors, and in what way rendered soulless? Whether we acknowledge it or not, most of us ask ourselves this question more frequently than we choose to answer it, but if we were to think a moment or two longer, it would become obvious that the kind of economic habits that are good for us are good for our communities, too. The obverse hardly needs stating.

Particularly in urban neighborhoods, where life is anchored less by class or occupational conformity than by the small places where we are made to feel at home, grassroots businesses and merchants are our lifeline. Bella Luna, Doyle's, the Santa Niño, and places like them humanize our material existence, connect us intimately to the functioning of our place. When we support our merchants, we are performing an act not unlike voting; entrusting our tastes, preferences, and needs to people we see every day. Sustenance becomes a reciprocal, an invested venture.

Villages work this way. Why shouldn't we? After all is said and done, a neighborhood's corner groceries and pharmacies are its informal communication centers, where news is exchanged, opinions swapped, and informal associational life flourishes or dies.

Until very recently, no one had a clue how to create such small economies if they didn't already exist—least of all in so-called urban gray areas of deterioration and decline. In Jamaica Plain it wasn't policy wonks who saw the light, it was the residents themselves.

In 1796 Joshua Seaver established the first store of its kind in Boston. Seaver's was the only general store along the coach route between Boston and Providence, and Seaver met every contingency, serving as depot master, post office representative, even policeman with a complete basement of cells. One charming local history recounts, "Here, also was . . . the favorite meeting-place of the townspeople to discuss local interests, engage in pleasantries, as well as exchange their coins for fine groceries, small wares, and farming utensils" (Harriet Manning Whitcomb, *Annals and Reminiscences of Jamaica Plain*. Cambridge: The Riverside Press, 1897). It was not just a good idea, in the days of geographic isolation, it was a practical necessity.

The town's bustle increased, as bustle does. Little except available space seemed to check Jamaica Plainers' enthusiasm for growth. A population that at its peak numbered fifty-five thousand maintained an astounding profusion of greengrocers, laundries, pharmacies, florists, and cafés in the single-story woodframe structures along narrow Centre Street. No longer was isolation the excuse for sustaining so many entrepreneurial gathering places. By the turn of the century, they helped to support the highly evolved life of the community. Businesses were proud of their role, and they took it seriously. They were vendors, yes, but first they were citizens. They helped underwrite Jamaica Plain's variety shows, skating parties, church bazaars, and parades. They offered hospitality, a home away from home. One tiny grocery, the Green/Elm Spa, claimed the coveted motto: "The Place Where Everybody Meets." So intimate were Centre Street's connections that if a store clerk changed his place of employment, he took out an ad, assuring customers, in the words of one, that he was "here at the new store to meet all old friends and customers." And it would remain thus for nearly another hundred years.

As recently as the sixties, I've been told, it was possible to spend the entire day down on Centre, shuffling from one moving conversation to the next until it was time to go home and make dinner. After breakfast at Barry's Deli, near the Monument, where the wags put away his famous Packman (six eggs, four strips of bacon, and two sausages), it was on to the barbershop for a second cup of coffee. If you had children in tow, you might stop at Erco's Toy Store, or Pearl's, for homemade fudge. There were nineteen pharmacies, nearly as many hardware stores, and any number of "lunches" to detain you along a mile-long expanse where nothing rose above one story except the old Winslow Building.

No day was complete without a stop into Hailer's. Its soda fountain was crowded morning and night. People perched on stools, or stood, sometimes two deep, and chatted while they waited for prescriptions to be filled, or they whiled an hour before paying for their toothpaste and a magazine. The Grossmans were frugal, hardworking, and content to make a modest enough living. They offered stolid, reliable stock, strawberry ice cream, and more. At Hailer's, neighborhood kids could find the odd job to stay out of trouble, poor families could buy at cost. And if someone was too sick to come in, their prescription was delivered, even in the middle of the night. The Grossmans were the salt of the earth, and no higher sobriquet could have flattered a Centre Street merchant.

But beginning in the mid-seventies, the lunch counter grew quieter and emptier. The old generation of customers and merchants around the pharmacy began to retire, and for the first time since Centre Street came to be, no one was interested in taking their place as small-time shopkeepers. Windows slowly grew dusty, the aisles and shelves leaner. Storefronts sat empty, sitting ducks for BB guns and vandals. Soon the inevitable grates of worn-out commercial strips turned up, blank patches of desertion from the Monument down to Jackson Square. And soon there was nothing for it, even for the Grossmans, but to close up shop and leave. An era had ended.

"Centre Street was closed up like a drum," reminisces resident Terry Bruce, as we sit over coffee at a local café. "I used to drive home some nights and wonder why I'd moved to this town. It looked like post–World War II Germany. The grates, and no streetlights."

She was right. I can remember driving down Centre at some point well into the eighties, after a friend had written a rave about a new hippie restaurant "out" in J.P. As I rolled down block after block of low, depressed storefronts that gave off the grim sheen of gunmetal, not even the homey sight of a pair of lace café curtains persuaded me to stop.

But along the side streets, unseen from Centre, the merchants and their customers had left behind a trove of grand old Victorians at stunningly cheap prices, and people like Terry were snapping them up. In their twenties, with money to spend, they'd come for a visit and fallen in love. Terry and her husband bought a fixer-upper on Sumner Hill several blocks from Centre.

"I can remember, we'd be out on ladders pounding and scraping," she tells me. "People would walk by and say, 'What a beautiful house. Where can I buy one?' So we'd turn them on to the older people who were selling their homes, and the whole thing blossomed."

The new architects, psychologists, law students, artists, and government workers who arrived with their moving vans and borrowed pickups were so preoccupied at first with replacing roofs and patching plaster walls that it hardly mattered that there wasn't any place to socialize outside of one another's homes. But they soon grew wistful for something to happen on Centre, to be able to stroll down and find the sort of café they loved in Harvard Square or SoHo.

Terry's sister's boyfriend talked about starting a bakery. And finally he did. He called it Today's Bread, and he rented space in a run-down storefront with glass windows that looked onto Centre Street. Terry gave him her croissant recipe—and J.P. loved it. So much so that within a year she'd taken over the business and, with it, begun life as a Jamaica Plain business-woman.

For three winters Terry operated Today's Bread without heat. On the floors above her were nothing but broken windows and pigeons. On the mornings when it had rained, before the crew got to work rolling out pastry, they had to disinfect the entire shop.

Finally, one day in 1984 the building was sold; Terry was able at last to fulfill her dream. She opened a street-level café with the enthusiastic support of the new owners, complete with small marble tables, café chairs, and exposed brick. Four years had gone by, and Today's Bread remained Centre Street's solitary gathering place for the new crowd. A bookshop, Food for Thought, came and went. A sporting goods store got off to a strong start, but it too eventually died. A florist and a framer's both went under. In their place came a CVS, a Videosmith, and a public assistance office. But still the grates remained.

Terry's croissants continued to draw a crowd. They were the

best anyone in town had tasted. It didn't matter to her that she wasn't making a great salary. "Just the fact that I could make somebody consistently happy day after day was enough for me then," she says. It was motive enough for sticking it out, hoping the commercial tide along Centre would turn.

Finally it did. A seafood restaurant opened a half block away. Farther down, the Centre Street Café offered brunches at its five small tables. Around the corner a crafts boutique opened, a trendy hair salon came in on South Street, and J.P. Licks began selling the best ice cream in Boston. People started to come in from as far away as Cambridge to stand in line for its white coffee and lemon ice.

Suddenly there were reasons to come down to Centre on a Saturday afternoon and return in the evening. You still had to go into the "city" or prosperous Brookline, or across the river to Cambridge, for books and chic clothes. But the feeling was growing that what people found on Centre in the trade-off was even better: a funky blend of Woolworth's and fresh juice bars, Thai food and hair-braiding salons. Young families, a growing population of gays and singles, and people from peripheral neighborhoods were generating a bustle again, and this was good news to Centre Street businesses.

At the other end of Centre, however, it was a very different story. Tony Barros could look east from his clothing shop in Hyde Square to a world of bodegas and botanicas, each one featuring the specialty of a distinct cuisine: Honduran, Venezuelan, Puerto Rican. The Cubans had been the first to arrive, working north to Jamaica Plain in the early seventies and establishing food shops and clothing boutiques that, even as poorer, less skilled groups from the Caribbean arrived, never lost their dominant market positions. The newer arrivals found their niches, often barnaclelike, in one-room bodegas, nail shops, and hair salons.

In many respects Tony could have been back home on the streets of Bani. His customers spoke little or no English and were dirt-poor. Only about half had finished grammar school. Many were employed in low-end jobs: janitorial services, house cleaners for the well-to-do on Moss Hill, nannies, bilingual hospital aides, and restaurant workers. And all day long among them, a steady stream of unemployed men—twice the percentage of Boston as a whole (17 compared with 8.5 percent) —paced the half-mile gauntlet of shops where they could cadge a smoke on credit, or news from home, and a plate of rice and beans.

Centre Street had broken down from a homogeneous commercial district into a mosaic of markets: from yuppies and progressive professionals to elderly blue-collar families, students, and working-class Latinos and African Americans. No longer was it "the place where everybody meets." Ethnic market distinctions had given rise to an unspoken segregation in residents' purchasing behavior.

Tony remembered living in a dirt-floored hovel in the Dominican Republic. After his father died, when Tony was six, he learned to scramble. Just in order to eat every day, he did anything he could think of to earn a few cents. When he was ten, his mother moved the family to Puerto Rico in hopes of a better life. There, Tony's nascent capitalism took on new forms. Before school, after school, and on weekends, he and his sister worked as itinerant salespeople. They roved the countryside with catalogues of goods that they would then deliver from the city outlets that supplied them. Life was hard, work was relentless and inevitable.

Tony didn't want his children to have to endure the hardships he had. Not for them a life confined to a poor barrio. In 1982, lured by his sister, he moved to Jamaica Plain. He sent his children to Catholic school and dressed them as well as he could afford to, in the hopes that their lives would be better than his had been. And in the thick of bodegas and familiar island sounds and smells, he opened a shop for women's and children's clothes.

His sateen dresses, tot-sized tuxedos, and deluxe First Communion dresses sold well to the Hispanic market, but he soon realized that to grow, he would need to capture a more varied clientele and perhaps move farther up Centre Street into Hyde Square. For the fact was that, while Latinos of all ages might stand in line at J.P. Licks Ice Cream on a Friday night or venture down to the Videosmith in Pondside, affluent white J.P. wasn't reversing the trend. No one from the pond area was coming down to the strip of shops between Hyde and Jackson Squares on a Saturday morning. For one thing, there were few goods or services to attract them. For another, it didn't feel safe.

Even Tony had to admit that it wasn't. What his fellow businessmen hadn't counted on, when they came north seeking opportunity, were the effects of the ever-escalating material expectations of American culture on their own children. Their young people were beginning to collide in frustration with the world outside the barrio. It had no job opportunities for them to move into, and they knew it. Instead, too many of them—enough to give an edge of danger to the streets—ended up like Eddy Ortega, in the limbo of rebellion, trading fast cars and gold-linked license plates for the old-time virtues of *respecto* and true machismo, so prized by their elders.

Crime was bad for business. Despite the elaborate monitoring and security devices Tony installed, he and the sixty other merchants along that part of Centre continued to suffer the effects of unabating street drug activity. Foot traffic fell off. The impulse buying upon which small-time businessmen rely, from women out walking with their children or workers on lunch break, dried up. Then one fall day in 1991, just as a small park down the street was to be dedicated by the mayor, a mother of four stepped out her door on the fringes of the festivities and was shot in broad daylight, the victim of a botched gang hit.

Though official Boston and federal agents responded immediately, with SWAT teams and offers of cash for informants, the damage had been done. Not for years would Hyde Square be seen as safe for business again.

From Kathie Mainzer's vantage point, the pattern was all too familiar. The establishment of a citizens' crime watch, reinforced by a demonstrable police presence, was a step in the right direction. But increased security alone wasn't going to rebuild Centre Street business, and she and merchants like Tony Barros knew it.

One day while she was driving through the Square, the old Los Felinos bar caught her eye. Gunshots and knifings had once been de rigueur at Los Felinos; 911 calls had been almost a nightly event, as its prostitutes and drug dealers spilled out into the street, adding their brew to what was just waiting in the darkness to be ignited. Now the bar was closed and the space it had occupied was an empty storefront in a forlorn corner next to a parking lot.

And Kathie, being Kathie, suddenly saw a pizzeria. She mentally festooned the sad, dusty windows with Christmas lights and strewed the smell of hot roasted peppers down the concrete steps and into the street. She envisioned crowds, mixed like her friends were, in a place that drew Jamaica Plain out and into the streets again to gather under gaslights on a swept sidewalk, for good food and street fairs and art shows and grassroots music. She'd occasionally dreamed such dreams in the past, of raising her daughter in a business, serving home-cooked food to friends, and making a business that was a kind of home in the world, an extended family, before leaving it to her daughter, a legacy of a well-lived life.

It was an old and quintessential American dream, she knew. She had no money and no credit history. But what better place to dream than on Centre Street in Jamaica Plain?

She went home and called her friend Charlie Rose. The two went way back, to the Citizens for Safety days. Charlie and his wife were devoted Jamaica Plainers, and Charlie, as deputy director of City Year, the national youth service organization, was deeply committed to urban youth. He was interested. So were Marcelo and Ivan Munoz, Chilean brothers who'd worked as chefs and played soccer with Kathie on an informal neighborhood league. Within weeks, the four had formed a partnership, and with the spirits of rank ingenues, they agreed that Kathie should approach Los Felinos's landlord to make their case. No other location would do.

Stavros Frantzis's offices were at the other end of town, not far from Today's Bread. That end of the street, with its upscale shops, offered a stark constrast to Hyde Square just a few blocks away. None of this was lost on Kathie the day she came down to meet Stavros Frantzis.

She climbed the stairs to Stavros's second-floor office. He himself opened the door. She was somewhat taken aback. His quarters weren't grand by any means, and they weren't sleazy in the style of old slumlords. The two rooms revealed instead a man of highly educated tastes and rumpled, masculine gentility. A long table dominated the room, covered with books of Greek art and contemporary architecture, literary novels, and a book of essays about his native village on the Aegean. Next to the bookcase hung a large canvas of an Expressionist nude. It was the office of a man who loved beauty more than luxury and had a curiosity as polyglot as he appeared to be. He was a sensualist, she decided, with a firm hand on the marketplace.

Stavros himself was gracious and imposing, a tall Greek with graying curls and a Roman profile and a penchant for open-necked shirts. He sat down and listened. Then he shook his head. No.

No stand-up, no take-out. Not in his properties. When he'd taken over that building, he'd kicked Los Felinos out. Now he was determined to let it stand vacant as long as he had to, until something genuinely good came along. Already he'd been approached by more beeper services than you could imagine, hoping to serve the drug trade, he explained in flawless, accented English. He was holding out for quality. A restaurant maybe, or nice little shops. . . .

He spoke at length of the agora, the marketplace, and its

centrality to community life. "The marketplace is the *most* important place," he told Kathie. "The agora was where people met and philosophized. You see this still in Africa, South America, and the Mediterranean. People use it not only to shop but to get together." Any Aegean fishing village knows more about the soul of community places than Americans do, he told her.

Kathie and her partners went back to the drawing board. They would do sit-down, with atmosphere and music and fancy salads. They would hang local art on the walls, and in the space out back, they would create an outdoor garden room. Stavros finally agreed.

Then they went looking for money. And they did what Tony Barros and generations of first-time businessmen had done before them: they asked family and friends for a thousand dollars apiece. They netted $55,000. Ivan and Marcelo purchased ovens and ordered food. Kathie and Charlie collected tables and chairs, cleaned the walls, and peeled years of boozy grime off the floors.

"We wanted to call ourselves something Italian that would work in a Spanish neighborhood and that English-speaking people would understand," says Kathie, who has joined me at my table.

One night, Charlie's wife, Carol, went out to see *Moonstruck* and came back with the winning inspiration.

Bella Luna. Beautiful moon. Serendipity, luck. When the moon hits your eye like a big pizza pie. It was perfect. An artist friend painted a food mural on a pizza pan: "Bella Luna Coming Soon." And they hung it in the window.

The partners worked feverishly the night before their grand opening, and finally, at midnight, they made their first pizza.

Ivan ceremoniously took it out of the oven, sliced it, and passed it around. Kathie took a bite and looked at the group.

"It tastes like shit," she told them.

It did. Something hadn't gone right. How can you ruin pizza? All that night they were sleepless. What was going to happen in the morning?

When they arrived the next morning, Ivan saw their mistake. In their excitement they'd failed to open the hood of the oven, to ensure proper ventilation—and a tender crust. It was fortuitous, because they already had a line. "We were completely swamped." She laughs. The pizza was a hit. "Any family member that was around ended up washing dishes."

In the months that followed, when she wasn't taking orders or running tables, Kathie got involved with the Hyde Square Merchants Association. She found them a hardworking but disheartened group that had little sense of mission and little experience in demanding the sorts of improvements in infrastructure—streetlights and garbage removal—that would upgrade the district and lure customers. Kathie knew organizing a lot better than she knew hard-crust pizza. There was work to be done in Hyde Square, and she was ready to roll up her sleeves.

The first challenge was to draw people down. She hit on the idea of organizing a Jamaica Plain "World's Fair" with booths, vendor tables representing the grab bag of cultures that were mingled around the Square, and kids' events. For a full day the square was closed to vehicles and took on the air of an itinerant carnival. And people came, lots of people. By day's end, no one had been shot. Not one had even been arrested. So this was how you went about it, Kathie thought. The following winter she ran a raffle from the restaurant for Christmas lights for the Square. Before she knew it, she was elected president of the Hyde Square Merchants Association.

The timing was right. Since Bella Luna opened, some dozen new businesses had hung up their signs. Momentum was beginning to pick up, and merchants were eager to come together as an organization and set new goals and priorities. Their demographics and challenges were clearly different from those of central Jamaica Plain. If Centre Street was going to recover its former vitality as the connective thread that joined diverse lives, these merchants would have to think more creatively than they had been up to that point.

Down in Terry Bruce's neighborhood, the source of Centre Street's revitalization had been the salaried professional jobs held by the residents who lived there. But at this end, the factory work that had supported earlier generations of customers was gone. In the late sixties and early seventies, the old breweries and shoe manufacturers down along the Stony Brook, which had once sent paychecks home in the pockets of hundreds of local people, had closed their doors. Their hulks idled on the backside of town. The irony was that a good number of newly arrived Latinos had come with factory skills, only to find that they couldn't market them in the area's transformed financial and service economy.

A number of years earlier, a group of local planners had begun to address the underlying problem of economic stasis in Hyde Square, the lack of jobs and entrepreneurial initiatives and capital. They evolved a vision: why not refit the largest of the vacant factories, the sixteen-building Hafenreffer Brewery, as an incubator for local, small-scale enterprises that could take advantage of local skills?

The neighborhood didn't need corporate monoliths to come in and occupy the industrial space, handing out a few token jobs like trinkets in exchange for the privilege of receiving tax breaks—a model that had been tried in urban gray areas around the country with little success, these planners believed. What urban pockets like Hyde Square did need, and would benefit greatly from, were a large number of small enterprises, all engaged in day-to-day interaction with the community, as employers, suppliers, and customers.

How do you go about filling in such a dream? You work with the materials at hand: with the people, their dreams, their needs, and your few but not insignificant advantages. You make the space habitable and offer cheap rents and common office services. Then you persuade small tortilla manufacturers that this is a profitable market, and pretzel and quick-turnaround sushi kitchens that it makes sense to be close to the airport and downtown restaurants. You pull in a variety of landscapers and pottery and woodworking and carpentry shops with access to financing and technical assistance.

What began as a small energy company that contracted with home owners to improve their insulation and weather-worthiness has grown today into a complex of some thirty businesses. They share common office services and a sense of ésprit de corps in their historic enclave of nineteenth-century brick structures. The largest of these, appropriately enough, is a microbrewery, the Samuel Adams Brewing Company, maker of Samuel Adams Beer. The brewery, along with businesses rang-ing from food production to small artisan shops, employs close to two hundred local people, a figure just shy of the heyday of the Hafenreffer.

By the early nineties the challenge facing Hyde Square merchants was how to capitalize on these and other encouraging trends in local employment and capture more of the estimated $45 million annually that residents were spending outside the neighborhood. How do you do this? You recognize the fine joinery by which the macroeconomics of a community is fitted to its Main Street, and while you concern yourself, as early generations of merchants did, with conditions on the street, you look for ways to encourage the intensification of local production and reinvestment into local businesses. The Hyde Square Merchants Association approached the city and the Neighborhood Development Council for technical advice on improving their business leadership skills. They actively and successfully helped promote the return of a major supermarket, and they negotiated changes in city parking and traffic patterns along congested streets.

Kathie is back at her pizza. When her tenure as association president ended, she was succeeded, to the enthusiasm of the entire Hyde Square community, by Tony Barros. Business is looking up, both for Tony and for Hyde Square. But Bella Luna remains unique. There isn't a quarter of Jamaica Plain, and far-flung daytrippers besides, who don't come down for pizza or to shop for groceries on Saturday morning and linger to see what's happening in the windows of Hyde Square's establishments.

No one has yet put in a soda fountain or a cappuccino maker, but that's just as well. In the protean place that we are today, any imported notions of the good life would miss the mark. What Hyde Square and Jamaica Plain needs are small places where we can be, in all manner of things, ourselves.

Kathie agrees with my ruminations. "This used to be a dangerous place. What we've accomplished here is job creation, economic development, job training, a lot of support for the arts. We've created thirty jobs. We pump over half a million dollars a year into the J.P. economy in salaries, supplies, and services. Flowers and printing and music—all of it. We change our art every six weeks to give local artists a nice opening. And we spend something like $14,000 a year on live music. Local musicians."

After three years in business, last year Bella Luna doubled in size. They expanded both their kitchen and their menu. They're open now for Sunday brunch and have a patio café. On an average night the fifteen-table eatery serves about 110 people in-house. And because demand is so brisk, with Stavros Frantzis's blessing, the restaurant does a huge delivery and take-out business. Annual volume sales run about $500,000, and this year Kathie's shooting for $750,000.

But perhaps the most dramatic expression of Bella Luna's intention to make Hyde Square "the place where everybody meets" is the garlic-infused crescent of tinseled moon that glimmers into the street long after the last customer has gone home.

A lot of the businesses around it still have grates on their windows, but Bella Luna specifically took a stand: no grates. Better by far to have bright lights and flowers, paper moons, and a large dollop of faith, twenty-four hours a day. Indeed, the faith seems to be justified. The pizzeria, where not so long ago knife fights were the nightly entertainment, has never had a single incident. Not one.

"You know," Kathie tells me, "if everybody extended from their own little window out to the street a sense of ownership, we'd all be better off. That's what makes a neighborhood safe, the sense of ownership."

ASSOCIATING

I BELONG TO A POETRY GROUP that meets every month or
so on the back porch of Meg and Kevin's house. Their neighborhood off Green Street used to belong to German brewers
and Irish shop clerks. Now its short winding streets are home
to folks like them, educated and single, second-generation
Americans, getting by on good hourly pay. My hair stylist lives
a few blocks away. Around the corner is a botanist I've con-
sulted several times about a tricky patch in my back yard.

At our meetings Kevin usually takes the makeshift hammock
in the corner. The rest of us occupy kitchen chairs that are in
romantic states of disrepair. For three hours we read and share
our work, and we discuss the book of poetry we've agreed to
study during the intervening month. Meg and Kevin have such
an insatiable appetite for poetry that they keep a volume of it
on their kitchen table beside the salt and pepper. They trek off
to readings in New York City as if they were just dropping in
on a party next door.

So devoted are they that several years ago they decided to do their own literary magazine. They gathered the best stuff they could get their hands on, some interesting images and an interview, xeroxed it onto brown paper bags, and stitched the whole thing together on Meg's sewing machine. The result was *Compost*, and it caused something of a stir in Boston's poetry scene. *Compost* is still around, a funky, downbeat hybrid of previously untranslated writers and emerging local artists that announces itself from this most hybridized of urban neighborhoods.

What we, in the group, have in common is a commitment to poetry that comes from any conceivable source. Otherwise we are students, part-time teachers, waitresses, and editors, and our purpose in gathering has more to do with love than with the yen for recognition, more with craft than with hubris. We drink coffee and munch on cake and bask in the civility of Sunday afternoons, and we observe that when you do what you do for purposes such as these, the view from even the narrowest sloping porch in the tightest corner of Jamaica Plain can be grand.

It's hard to estimate exactly how many small groups like ours exist here because they don't advertise. I know of several Puerto Rican and Venezuelan folk dance groups, a gay men's dinner club, a women's spirituality group, and a ladies' investment club. There is a Friends of the Cemetery group, chess clubs, and meditation circles.

And these are just the informal organizations. Open any issue of the paper, and you'll see hundreds more. Jamaica Plain has more active neighborhood associations than any other neighborhood in Boston, more than twice as many crime watches, and conservatively three active social justice or mission groups for every church. To skate even lightly across the sea of social analysis these days, it is clear that in our associational zeal, we are aberrant. Study after study informs us that Americans' capacity to enter into voluntary association, the glue that de Tocqueville considered the single most significant fact in our success as a participatory democracy, has so dried and flaked and been so blown apart by antagonistic chemistries that you can hardly find traces of it left.

Our problem here is just the opposite. Except for working downtown, whole months can go by without our having to leave the heart of the place we've constructed out of the adhesive of common pleasures and whim.

How has it happened that we have given the lie to the sociologists' remorse? I'd like to think our fusion stew is the distant legacy of Emily Balch and the ladies of the Needle Woman's Friend Society, but this is a fancy located more in sentiment than sense.

To answer this question, I set out on a visit to one of our venerables. She is a woman not without controversy, for anything else would not suit us here. But for seventy-three years neither head colds nor lost political battles have put her off her habit of striding hip-deep into the human densities. She still shows up at most of the meetings, teaches Sunday school every week, and takes strangers in off the street. I suspect that, like a patient spider, she has as keen a sense as anyone now living of why, in spite of our often majestic differences, we seem to continue to prefer one another's company to the infinite alternatives.

The day is warm and sunny as I drive down to the Southwest

Corridor. Landscaped now and lush, its playgrounds filled with children and mothers and small bands from the local day cares, it's hard to remember when it was a graveyard of homes and of all that seemed to have died with them. I cruise past, toward Egleston Square. After years of reeling from the effects of the corridor and neighborhood disinvestment, people are working hard to create a similar revival here.

Just off the Square, I turn into a side street and park. Ruth Parker's house is the first on the left. In the morning sun several Hispanic men are working on cars. Shirtless, in their twenties, they see all that goes on down on Washington. In silence or to the blare of salsa, they tinker with tires or spark plugs. They watch.

On a porch just wide enough to hold a folding chair, Ruth's blinds are drawn. But an old mongrel is watching, too, and now she comes charging along the chain-link fence. This wasn't exactly what I had in mind when I thought of Ruth Parker. But then, I wasn't sure just what I did have in mind, until a distant voice, muffled, hastens forward with an aging, matter-of-fact bustle.

To me: "Go on in, go on in!"

And to the dog: "Daisy!"

The door, to my surprise, is open. The house, still. Then Ruth appears.

"She wouldn't hurt a flea—just got a bad tooth," she explains apologetically. Her gray hair is cropped close, and she has on workaday blue knit slacks and a white T. Nothing in Ruth Parker strains for effect. One senses this instantly. Direct, yes, kindly, yes. Forceful. She so precisely fits the image that I didn't even know I'd had of her that I don't have to look long to fix her in memory.

We settle in a toile twilight of figurines and draped furnishings, and I discover that I am in one of those old glories, a home with enough space for graciousness but none for pretension. Ruth was born in this house in 1923 and grew up among its sitting rooms and siblings and the various neighbors who passed through its upper altitudes for months at a time when times were rough and jobs scarce. It was an intimate kingdom of purposes and orders, overseen by a strong-willed English mother and her doting Irish husband.

"Everybody could do something, and everybody had something to do," Ruth recalls. As soon as she could walk, she was expected to clean the front and back stairs, just as her brother was to sweep the wooden sidewalk out in front and take it up to be painted each spring. Along the strand of such tasks, the days strung themselves into weeks, all wending toward Friday, baking day, and the inviolate ritual of Saturday.

Saturday was the day that the door was opened and the world of the neighborhood was invited in. Ruth would help pass the cake, then sit with the other children at the small table set for them against the wall in the dining room. From there she listened to the tales and exploits and barefaced lies with which the adults entertained one another, making life in a strange land hospitable.

"It would be Annie Lynch—she never married—Kathleen and John, who'd just lost Teresa, and maybe my mother's friends around the corner on Dixwell. I can remember all the laughter," she says. "No one was blood relations, strictly speaking, but they were all family. Everybody was there. Nobody had anything. Everybody was happy."

The family next door was Italian. Next were Germans. Next to them lived Italians, and lastly another Irishman. On the other side of the street were Greeks and Russian Jews—all of them searching for connections in a place without familiar landmarks or customs.

As Ruth lapses into silence, I think of how among these rooms she learned the first and most important lesson about joining: that it isn't a taking and it isn't a giving. It is a sharing, the capacity to open up spaces in which otherness becomes the gift that enters and moves and shapes affinity. It isn't the game of bridge or bowling. It is the mind-set, the willingness to raise the roofbeams and push into the attic to make a suitably generous space for all that cannot be expected, for the magic and the muddle of being human together. It is hospitality in a world of strangers where nothing else is certain.

Clubs were far too formal a shape for this hospitality to take. People made the common rooms of life out of the little they had—their children, work, and church. When the young people put on a play down at the church or held a raffle for a school dictionary, everybody in the neighborhood bought tickets. When someone's child needed a First Communion dress or a winter coat, mothers would forage in the closets at home.

"My brother is gone now," Ruth speaks again, breaking the silence. "He took with him the secret of where he took the pots of soup at night. But now—I'm seventy-four—now I meet people who tell me, 'Your mother fed us.' Or, 'Didn't you know that the only Christmas presents we ever got were from your mother?' "

One day a friend grabs the golden ring, the next is struck down by illness. In the best of all worlds, there is a seamlessness to associational life, between compassion and respect, imagination and need. There is a moving beyond easy laughter to genuine meetings. This business of meetings can be raw and gravely uncertain ground. Is all this really necessary to dwell together well in a place? It is. It is the piece that J.P.'s nineteenth-century women demanded of themselves and one another. It is the piece we rarely hear spoken of today.

Politics was a separate realm. Except where it touched down into that most common of rooms, the street, with its rallies and back-of-the-trick stump speeches—politics didn't enter into the motivating principles of local associations. Ruth and her friends wouldn't dream of taking on a particular policy or putting up an opposition candidate. For thirty years in Jamaica Plain there was "the man to see." Jimmy Craven was Jamaica Plain's state rep, a powerful, pugnacious, unyielding statesman of the old ward tradition. He dispensed jobs and public contracts, aided the schools, and voted with the unions and for a quarter of a century went uncontested. And so long as the bars in the Square kept their patrons in line, there was nothing, in Ruth's words, "to get hairy about."

As a result, talent shows and benefit dances continued to figure far more prominently in the community life than did the promotion of local candidates or platforms or ward committees. Energies were focused on the quality of daily life. The "angels of the house," at large on the streets and in the markets and schools, were disposed to put their energies into the town's spirit rather than its will.

Ruth married, and she and her husband took up residence together in the family home. She rode the elevated downtown to the First National Bank, where she worked. Returning to the fold of family and street life, she walked each evening in Franklin Park and was a staunch and loyal resident of Egleston Square, one of many who, though they held no official power, possessed an authority about local affairs that, as long as everything worked, rendered elected service if not irrelevant, then unnecessary—even redundant. They knew where to go to get the things done that needed to be done, and for the rest they were content to enrich local life in humble grassroots ways.

The biggest event of the year was still midnight Mass at the Catholic church on Christmas Eve. And the most profound pleasure was derived from the hours not at all unlike those we spend on Sunday afternoons at Meg and Kevin's house.

"This time of year, summertime, after supper, everybody went outdoors. The men would congregate and talk ball game, things like that. The women would be wherever the children were—or wherever your mother was, that's where you had to play. They'd socialize that way," Ruth says softly. "And it was a wonderful way."

I'd expected the voice of old Jamaica Plain to be more—well, guarded, perhaps, the way old-timers I've known in other places experienced their personal history as a category of loss.

In the Southwest Corridor debacle, Ruth and her cronies were on the losing side, in part because their vision wasn't in step with J.P.'s changing tides but in greater part because the older political style was doomed in an arena of big-power politics. Like everything else about the public life of association that had been lived up to in her day, it was accommodationist, not confrontationalist. If a highway had been decreed, so be it. The most advisable tactic under the circumstances was to scurry and rescue as much as possible of what had been, to shore up streets and congregations, attitudes and habits, against the tide of inevitable change.

Four streets away lived a member of the new breed. Younger, savvier, Winky Cloherty found herself so entirely swept up in the matter of the highway that there wasn't a corner of her life that wasn't politicized. If Ruth's world was something of a loose and rambling manse, Winky's was more like a cell.

In time and by the lights of its political assumptions and values, the cause gradually enveloped more and more areas of life. A defeated highway became wrapped up with the idea of day care centers, better schools, neighborhood organizations, and local housing politics.

Hundreds of movements and causes in American society have come and gone in precisely this fashion. They invariably throw into dramatic relief the weakness of Ruth's way of life, its docility, its ambiguities, and its inability to mount an effective defense of itself for lack of a sufficiently broad political perspective. Focused, these causes expose the generally distracted path of most of mankind most of the time, and they invite a powerful kind of association that, if it isn't rooted in hospitality, offers wanderers strength and a sanctuary against the casual victimization and entropy of history.

It is heady stuff, these causes, but if they remain only that —intellectual, focused, self-justifying—they are doomed, as hundreds of them have proven to be. For association to matter, to amount to anything, focus must marry repetition. Ideas need to be lived. Together, focus and repetition open groups up to hospitality, and it is here, at this nexus, that the transformative potential of their new visions emerge.

It is the old work of hospitality in a different guise, and it saved Jamaica Plain from mere opportunistic ideology. Winky and her new friends envisioned living in a place full of public ritual and local creativity where children and new immigrant groups felt welcomed with their traditions. And they were committed to living out the implications. When she wasn't attending meetings, she was hosting mothers' groups and organizing picnics and weekend cocktail parties for the newcomers in town.

"We socialized a lot," Winky once told me. "You look today at the renovation of playgrounds, the neighborhood clinics. There was a community of interest that sustained these efforts. Our social life was built on discussing these new ideas."

It meant moving the walls of the attic. One new mother in town began to gather a group of other mothers around the sewing machine in her attic. For weeks, while the children played at their feet, these women created the kind of hands-on crafts and celebrations they wanted their children to know. They manufactured small rag dolls and puzzles, invented games and prizes, gifts and poems—favors that cost pennies but bound them to one another in a way no store-bought presents ever could.

Around life's daily happenings a new life was built. The community gardens spawned seasonal festivals, more community gardens, neighborhood associations, school projects, crime watches, neighborhood councils, and in time new life for and in churches.

The old power structure was gone, replaced by progressive state representatives and a strongly progressive ward committee; the old certainties vanished. But the old behaviors by which community was created and sustained for aeons proved to hold their value. Once the newcomers confronted the very real threat of the highway to their sense of place, they looked within—and found something that old-timers like Ruth Parker had always known: there is a richness to sustaining engagement in a place that can be better than anything gets.

The experiences they shared had created rich common rooms, not the kind you walk away from or fade away from, because they hold so much of the emotional grain. You raise your children only once, get the chance to touch a place deeply only once in a lifetime. And where you have worked to bring a street, a block, a little place "back," you are invested in ways that make leaving, or any more superficially attractive alternative, almost inconceivable.

Joseph Campbell, writing about the character of the active life, by which we may reasonably assume he meant the life of association, once had this to say: "What we are seeking is an experience of being alive, so that our life experiences on the purely physical plane will have resonances with our innermost being and reality, so that we actually feel the rapture of being alive. That's what it's finally all about."

As for Ruth Parker, who knew all about the rapture of being alive, political defeat could never pull down the enduring verities. She continued to teach Sunday school, go to meetings, speak out on neighborhood crime and development issues, and hobnob with neighbors. Just recently, she has started a new neighborhood organization. Those who get together on her block the first Tuesday of the month for coffee and conversation are Ecuadoran, Columbian, and Puerto Rican rather than Italian and Greek. They hold potlucks and cookouts, share stories, and keep an eye on one another's children. In between, they tackle the problems of community life that haven't changed much in fifty years, despite altered ideologies: liquor licenses, public decency, and the ties of affection. And they can take some credit for the fact that together they are able to do more than they could alone: there is decidedly less tension in the Square than there was even a year ago. Though the drugs aren't entirely gone, the gangs are.

Throughout town the old ways are alive and well. Not long ago, while thinking about them, I bumped into Deborah Galiga down on Centre Street. Deborah is a quintessential new-timer. She runs a crafts school out of John Eliot's original one-room schoolhouse. The school offers classes in carpentry, bookmaking, sewing, stained glass, and upholstery to community members of all ages. On the side, she is a professional musician.

When she moved to Jamaica Plain ten years ago, Deborah

was looking to meet piano students and get gigs for her band. A friend talked her into helping run the fledgling arts center. Deborah booked programs and generally kept track of things. In the process she met lots of artists, local business people, and parents and kids. Before long she was moonlighting at the keyboard, tuning pianos, teaching lessons, and performing.

But when a salaried job offer downtown came her way, it seemed too good to turn down. She passed her students off to another local woman and became a commuter. Now in her spare time, at night and on weekends, she tried to stay in touch with the neighborhood by interviewing for the *Jamaica Plain Arts News*, a monthly tabloid on artists and trends. Her circle of acquaintances expanded. She met members of crime watches that had blossomed into more creative affairs. Some did annual block parties, others ran child-care co-ops. And she realized how much she missed being in the neighborhood day after day.

These days, when she isn't scheduling classes and securing teachers, she's out and about in town again, soliciting donations, talking to school groups, running open houses. Last year Deborah ran for her second term on the neighborhood council and won. She sits on the parks and human services committee, where she works on health care and grassroots anti-drug projects in the community.

"I'm a perfect example of a person who moves in many realms," she says. "And lots of people in Jamaica Plain are like that."

It is true.

Several fellow council members have run for higher public office; others are on the board of the Eliot Street School.

Scratch a neighborhood association member, and you'll discover someone with another local commitment: a music group, a tutoring project, or an expertise in local lore. Together they sustain the vim of our associations and the quality of life here, that intensity of contact that still gives us more in common and more of value than anything the "outside world" can provide.

Like a small independent republic existing beside a colonial power, we have not so much a bunker mentality as an awareness that what is small and responsive to the will of its members is worth its weight in gold. Old-timers don't forget that much of the new community arose in response to external threats to its well-being and grew from there. The state highway, the drug trade, and unresponsive government agencies, all in their time, have made an end run on the delicate web of relationships that we call our life.

Defense is an underrated notion. It triggers visions of redneck towns and ethnic intolerance, small-mindedness and meanness. And yet we need but look at the Amish, the Mennonites, Seventh-Day Adventists, and monastic communities to see that it is not just finicky rules that set them apart and lend them an enviable centeredness. It is their faithfulness to values and beliefs worth defending through a careful balance of discipline, mutual support, and celebration.

Buddhists are quick to advise novices that it is best to study just one of the religion's three thousand possible iterations. Even when confusion and frustration set in, it is a far better thing to stick with the muddle than to seek satisfaction in a more superficially accessible experience of insight. The Benedictines in their monasteries take a vow of stability. Staying put doesn't make you narrow, this wisdom says; it gives you depth.

This is the philosophy of place. Those who adopt it dig in, heel and soul. They take the long view of the challenge of community in our time, recognizing the seductions of a cosmopolitanism that says small and local don't matter, that where we live and who we live among are less important than what we own, buy, and do for a living. The antidote, wildly countercultural and authenticating and freeing, is association. Preserving the integrity of small and diverse places, our rose lovers' clubs and our poetry groups and our salsa ensembles, is the best antidote we have to the generic consumerist culture that threatens to swallow us body and soul, in one greedy gulp.

Or to put it another way, in a world where nothing but this is certain, our treasure is one another.

CELEBRATING

—·—·—·—·—·—·—·—·—·—·—·—·—

IT IS GRIM. Wet sidewalks and threatening skies. By the Monument a brace of motorcycle police officers cross their arms and study the clouds. Overtime or not, a two-hour trek through cold rain is no one's idea of easy pool money.

But the Wake Up the Earth Festival has already been postponed once. Last year, when the rain date proved as soggy as the original, the organizers called the thing off, but residents had gathered spontaneously anyway, carrying out a kind of people's festival—which is what our annual street fair is all about to begin with—causing no end of havoc among disgruntled vendors and confused traffic patrols.

At six o'clock this morning, Gina Rheault rose and walked over to the old German Club on Danforth Street. The Schul Verein used to hold weekly dance nights and a crowded calendar of cultural offerings for members. Then it lay idle for a good ten years, gathering dust and the usual code violations. These days, without substantial improvements, it has found a new life as the festival's temporary command center. And this morning, as the pigeons began to wake and flap around on the flat tar roof next door, Gina pushed into the cavernous gloom and recorded a chipper message on the answering machine. The festival was on.

But by eight-thirty her confidence was sagging. Down at the fairgrounds, she watched with dismay as her chalk marks for the vendors' booths were washed away as quickly as she could set them down. The skies had opened, and it was teeming. Her first thought was to leave town as quickly and as quietly as possible and return to the Colorado hamlet where she'd spent the last year as a ski-bum anthropologist working at a hotel and learning the ways of small-town life.

Months of preparation had gone into pulling the festival day parade together once again: bands and banners, huge papier-mâché puppets and stilt dancers, costumes and quilt squares, and improv political theater. The Latina women in the neighborhood had spent days cooking the pans of rice and beans they would be selling. Endless hours had gone into scheduling the music and children's activities for the daylong event. Up until this morning, the lessons gained in a town of two hundred had held her in good stead: if anything about Jamaica Plain was small town, it was the Wake Up the Earth Festival. But there is no wisdom that can take account of weather. Not with people in a mind to party, anyway.

At eleven I venture out, curious to see what intrepid souls other than the police have elected to flout the skies. At the street corners around the Monument, I come upon the usual small knots of preteens, black, white, and Latino, tapping their feet, or drums, or twirling on their in-line skates with their usual nonchalant volatility. A few couples with young children smile at nothing in particular with forced optimism.

Disappointed, I'm about to hunt down a cup of coffee when I bump into an acquaintance, a local school committee member who works with high school dropouts during the week over in Somerville. Her nine-year-old son has braced himself against one of the pillars of the town hall and is struggling into a pair of stilts.

"He made them himself," she tells me proudly, craning her neck as he rises four feet above our heads. "The costume, too."

I crane as well, and as he staggers toward the parade's theoretical starting line, I admire the assemblage of crutches and two-by-fours, flannel shirts and tablecloths that his mother, Sue, has surrendered to the cause.

"He wants me to spot him," she says apologetically. "But Saturday mornings are my only time to get any paperwork done." All the same, she doesn't leave.

We mosey over to the limp carcass of a cloth-and-paper dragon. The dragon is the parade's perennial main attraction, leading the way down Centre Street to the fairgrounds along Southwest Corridor Park, a grimacing mélange of green, orange, and yellow that at its conception satisfied some long-graduated fourth-grade class at the Agassiz Elementary School with its menace and terror. As we stand there, taking it in again like a long-lost friend, a man in jeans and a Hawaiian shirt saunters over. He wonders out loud whether there will be enough children to supply its prodigious length with legs. We cast an eye around. It looks dubious.

The cops still hang, the teens in their rangy plaits still lean against fences and lampposts. Banners and puppets lie wilting on the damp sidewalks. It is a scene of brief but weary catastrophe. Luckily, I think, Gina isn't here. She's still at the fairgrounds. This would be the final straw.

It is cold and getting on toward lunch, and I still haven't had my coffee. I'm about to leave when, suddenly, behind us, in front of us, in the streets, drums on some unseen cue are beating an indescribable timbre into the morning air.

It is a rousting, subdural and green. My blood courses a little faster as I look around, my somnolence pierced apart by the broad, brassy pulse of expectancy. There are steel drums and skin drums and primitive gourds that sound like dry leaves in a rainstorm. They are being struck by sticks and bones and hands, but mostly by hands, and so they have the visceral impact of chant. I find myself lulled by their urgency, so arresting yet so strangely comforting.

We are wide awake now, even if the earth hasn't quite come around, and the toddlers who have been aimlessly wheeling their tricycles in the street waiting for something to happen are shooed to the side so that the men in blue can prepare nothing less than the enchantment of Centre Street.

A graceful young dancer appears on stilts, trailing rainbow streamers from her wrists. She leads us off, followed by my friend's son. Behind them two women step up, one young and one old. They bear between them the hand-painted festival banner that's seen us through countless Mays.

An entire cast of characters has materialized, and with the usual anarchistic touches that give anything that happens in this town its charm, a parade is hobbled into being. A mariachi

band, in red boleros and polished brass, falls into line. Not far
behind, in torn jeans and ragged hats, comes an all-female
band, full of spit and a beat so hot that they stop sidewalk traffic
in its tracks and pull even the faint of heart into their wake.

This is nothing if not a participatory event. From the sidewalk people cheer and wave, forget about their errands, and
join the ragtag procession. Children in butterfly costumes hold
hands with bearded, aging hippies. A Vietnamese girl parades
in solitary splendor, showing off her magnificent traditional
beaded gown. A group of retarded adults in gaily decorated
hats moves in a cluster, happily playing kazoos. Masked grown-
ups go by, some carrying maypoles, some oversize puppets.
There are dogs and saxophones, a few wheelchairs, and perhaps
most memorably a capacious woman who wears a tie-dyed bed-
sheet and a daisy-chain crown and stands in the street handing
out a flower to everyone who passes her by.

Centre Street has never looked better than it does on this
morning, with the human garland of sound and color and fancy.
Even the pavement seems to be dancing. As we leave the stolid
chic of Pondside and make our way down into Hyde Square,
the moving column swings ever more gaily, lengthens, and
thickens. Traffic by now is reduced to a single lane and often
stalls. Paraders pass their surplus of daisies through the windows of idling cars.

Hispanic men smile as we pass by, standing in clusters close
to the buildings, smoking and talking among themselves. Bless-
ings on us. *Santos. Idolos.* But their wives and children are not
nearly so remote. Two Puerto Rican boys just back from softball practice toss their balls to their father and fold in alongside

us, running. The older ones raise their cans of soda and grin, then fall in happily, revelers, dancers, like most of us as Saturday finds us, in sneakers and jeans, hopeful of a little magic, a little laughter, a little sunshine. It isn't too much to expect, really, after so long and gray a northern winter.

In half an hour we reach the swarming bodegas. People wave and laugh, joining in the festive air. This is the day when even the Anglos touch down into the wild confraternity of the bacchanal; it is a happy day.

Just ahead are the fourteen-story towers of the Bromley-Heath projects. Beyond them Centre Street ends, somewhat ignobly, in subway tracks and a busy access road. The parade will turn and follow a patchwork of city-controlled land and open lots to the area set aside for the day's events. At the corner a clutch of Hispanic children grin shyly and wave from behind heavily grated and locked windows. Suddenly the smallest of them throws caution to the wind. She flings open the sash and, to the assembled concatenation of pounding cymbals and bells, gongs and deafening brass, tosses out her own small and accented contribution, "Hello! Hello! Hello!"

I turn to take us in. It *is* dazzling. A phalanx of strollers and beaming Spanish grandmothers have worked themselves up to the head of the parade. And towering above them, two city blocks back, rears the proud, defiant grin of the resurrected dragon.

Back in February, while snow still clogged the narrower passes all over town, Gina had sat down and made a list.

Site
Parade
Vendors
Music
Kids' Activities

She was confident. She had precedent on her side. For years
the general elements of the festival had remained the same.
In the past each had been handled by a seasoned volunteer
under the aegis of the festival's creator, Femke Rosenbaum.
But last year for the first time, Femke and the old-timers had
gotten together and decided they ought to have a general coordinator. It seemed sensible. Even though the event had been
going on for so many years that parts of it, like the drums,
seemed to happen of their own accord, some felt they'd been
running on luck for a while. All sorts of things could go wrong
or fall through the cracks. Or the old stalwarts could cease to
participate for one reason or another. And because no part of
the logistics had ever been written down, where would they
be?

Hope Haff had done it last year. She was one of the originals;
she went way back in the community. Gina wasn't. She'd lived
in J.P. for only six months. Where Hope had emerged from
the freewheeling past and could maneuver in its style, Gina
had a background in corporate sales, with visions of orderly
time lines and a firm budget. Everyone thought it was a good
match. Even Hope, better organized than most and an adept
of the local zeitgeist, had torn her hair out over the unexpected
details. Gina was determined to avoid that. Despite her ingenue
rank, she knew well enough that in the universe of art and

nature, and certainly in the universe of Jamaica Plain, nothing was cast in stone.

So she sat down and said, okay. We have six weeks to pull this off. Logically, what are all the things that have to get done in order for this to take place? She started from the day of the festival and moved backward, mapping out deadlines, limning a schedule. It looked possible.

It looked possible because, for starters, Hope would be co-ordinating the parade. And another bit of invaluable luck walked through the door in the person of Greg Allen. Greg had spent his whole life in J.P. and was plugged into its prodigal, often rivalrous music scene. Gina offered to divide her salary in exchange for letting him handle the estimated twenty groups who wanted to perform sometime the day of the festival.

She transformed a room in her house into an office. She hooked up a separate phone line. She brought in a portable computer and scanner.

Gina liked the feel of meetings, their shape and order. So she called one. The old volunteer list had about fifty names on it. She called them all by phone and let them know when to show up.

But when only five people appeared, she got to thinking. She seemed, with all of her organization and diligence and efforts to keep plans on track, to be operating in a parallel universe to the unseen forces of local lore and tradition. A day didn't go by that she didn't discover one more detail that had escaped her attention. Increasingly, things were happening from some independent volition, quite beyond the scope of her control.

Finally one day, in an exercised state, she asked Hope, "Who *are* we working with? I've been here six months, and this person has been here twenty years and is so in tune with what's going on that it doesn't even occur to them that they need to talk to me!"

Hope, on the other end of the line, just smiled.

Twenty years ago there was nothing. No parade, and only demolished housing and littered open land, and two communities, one black, one white, in estrangement on either side of it. The endless strife and politicking over the disposition of the land had raised many questions about race, unequal voices, and the oppression of poor people at the hands of big bureaucracies. But the questions remained unanswered. In the aftershocks the people didn't know what to do to heal, or even whether it was possible to heal. They had no place to put their rage and grief and sense of betrayal; no traditions, or common institutions through which they could repair the rents. What once had been here in the way of such things had slipped out of common use.

But two newcomers to town had arrived with a language of customs that reached far back in time, older than American ways, to European and pagan agrarian rituals. Femke was one of them. She had grown up in Holland, where the year was punctuated by feast days and observances, like the Feast of Saint Martin, when children hollowed out sugar beets and went door-to-door singing old English songs and asking for wood or a piece of turf to keep warm.

When she moved to Jamaica Plain in 1974, Femke brought her memories with her. Soon she was staging art-making days and puppet shows and spur-of-the-moment festivals. Her warmth and charisma drew neighborhood children to her house and in time won over their mothers, as well. Their Saint Nich-

olas Day observance became so popular that they were invited
to run it at the local grammar school, and in time some 350 children in the community and their parents took part each year.

That was as far as it went, until Femke met the other newcomer, a folklorist. Twice each year, at Christmas and again in
the spring, this woman hosted small folklore rituals for friends
at her home. Femke attended one of her spring events. It began with "priests" going out into the woods and bringing back
greens from the budding boughs. They brought the returning
spring, and as they moved among the group, they touched people with its first manifestations. Then drums woke up the earth,
and bells purified the air, and a series of ecstatic dances acted
as a sort of physical prayer. The higher one danced, the higher
the crops would grow.

It was an ancient English rite, and Femke was enthralled.
Many things came together in her mind.

"I thought, well, this is nice to do with a group of friends,"
she'd once told me. "But really, this was something that was
done by the whole community, not just by a few families. I
started thinking, wouldn't it be nice if we did this with the
whole community—re-creating agrarian rituals in an urban
setting?"

As she mulled all this over, the site became obvious and so
did the configuration of the event. Two parades, one from Jamaica Plain and one from Roxbury, would meet halfway on the
embittered land. Together, people would spend the day in celebration.

Her network of women friends came through. They sewed
costumes and made banners. Femke called on Puerto Rican
grandmothers who taught folkloric dance, and a Bolivian

woman made piñatas. She tapped whoever she could find. Across the way in Roxbury, a woman named Fatima Paine rousted up some African drummers.

On that first Saturday in May 1977, they came. Twirling batons, drumming, in elaborate costumes, with exotic dishes of food, and lots of music, and nubile local beauties displayed on top of freshly washed cars. It was magical and authentic, in a neighborhood that drew its cultural sources not from the established rhythms of a long-standing agrarian place but, like generations of urban dwellers before them, from the cities of Africa, South America, Europe.

There hasn't been a May since then that the festival hasn't taken place.

Now the parade has arrived at the fairground, and its parts disbanded into a loose and high-spirited mob. Gina stands taking it all in. The clouds have lifted, and miraculously the sky is holding. And she has learned something about this place that cherishes its rituals. It has happened as it always has, not because of her but because of a durable and inarticulated faith. The normally unpeopled stretch of parkland has metamorphosed into a campy bazaar. As far as the eye can see, vendors and merchants snake along the pavement, selling everything from tamales to alternative education, Honduran hats to hand-painted pottery, herbals to hair wraps. At the entrance to the park, local organizations have set up tables with literature and sign-up sheets. A Caribbean woman hawking handmade aphrodisiacs has inexplicably made her way into the mix. Next to her a Massachusetts Cannabis Reform Coalition representative hands out literature to all who will take it, a lei of marijuana leaves dangling from his neck. Beside him sit the stately members of the J.P. Historical Society, with their orderly and circumspect stacks of bibliographical source lists and street maps.

And people are buying. Vast plates of rice and beans waft past. Folks stop to chat with the performers, kids run after dogs and wend around knots of neighbors in turns of bike and skates. Over the years the festival has grown and been modified ever so slightly, depending on the year's vintage of enthusiasts. But there are always one or two of the old chestnuts. This year a political theater troupe is presenting a continuous monologue on global violence. There is the *teatro popular*, a small grassy space holding a black microphone for anyone so moved to mount their soapboxes. And as always, there is the May Day mural, an elaborate Marxist narration of world and J.P. history, recounted by various fantastical creatures.

Having walked the length of the grounds, I turn and retrace my steps. From a distance I spy my son, who has just arrived and is tethered to his father's hand like a kite in a gale. He points, he tugs. He wants it all, now. We make a long and lingering tour of the food tables before settling on refried rice and pork curd. We turn down a request for a wooden flute but assent to buying a Guatemalan hat so tall it nearly topples him. In the crowd we recognize familiar faces, folks we don't see every day. It is a good time to catch up with friends from Moss Hill, the stained-glass artist who lives on St. John's, Christine Cooper from the boathouse, Winky Cloherty, and resting somewhat off to the side on a bench in the tot lot, Deborah Galiga, a bemused look on her face.

Later in the day, there will be face painting and jugglers,

ethnic dancers and storytelling. But now on the bank just above us, children duck in and out of a floral maze. Without a lot of choice, we follow our leader, and for the better part of the afternoon, he is stuck in the maze. It is actually a spiraling labyrinth. We chat with more passing friends while he dashes from crepe-paper daisy to daisy, mesmerized by this game that, drawing him past the same landmarks curve after delicious curve, also bears him deeper in some thrilling interior direction. It is a sensation at once physical and incorporeal, and as he spins, he laughs, thrilled to be so transported. How like this day, I think, in the otherwise disjunct turnings of our year. In spite of its dogged anarchies, it allows us to touch once again the common seed that has slept for a season, the way all things tend to do, nodding off in the middle of the music. With its return, we are reconstructed, wakened again as a wayward tribe with a certain amount of faith in the common enterprise.

We are ritualistic creatures, after all. In the absence of life-affirming rituals, we will make our own, and there is no guarantee, lacking such common troth, that they will be particularly good for us. I know several women who routinely regurgitate most of what they eat, or shop until they're numb. I know men who drink or work or kill too much. In the matter of our rituals, there is no contest: make the vessel large, the universe says, and keep it true. Large enough to hold your all and turn you toward the light, and at its quiet, beating center, awaken you to the fact of being alive, and companioned, in the labyrinth.

Other children, more adept at the play than he, pass my son, crisscrossing in and out. At first this sends him into dizzy confusion. He halts, blinks, and stares. But soon he is crowing with each startling recognition. He is too young to know the story of this day. But he will grow into it with the years, elaborating with a young man's mind on what his body already senses— that there is a center to his ever changing and unpredictable world that will hold him in its fastness, to the life here into which each day he awakens and turns again.

The sky has held, and the cold has brought us closer than we otherwise would have been, huddled in windbreakers and winter blazers. Greg Allen has done himself proud. We've watched a rap group that attracted a respectable crowd of the neighborhood's teens, half admiring, half cool, along the lip of grass just above the bandstand. We have heard an old-time gospel group from one of the churches nearby. Elsewhere, basketball courts and open patches of grass have become makeshift stages and concert halls. Saxophonists, drummers, a cappella singers, and a ragtime band—some booked for the day and some simply moved—regale us. We sit close to one another on the low concrete walls that serve as backstops, chatting and listening and keeping one another's kids away from the amplifier lines. The troop in the maze has migrated to the maypoles. They wrap ribbons and tumble over picnic blankets and dogs; they chase one another up the ladders and down the slides of the little playground.

At five o'clock we fold up tables and banners, unsold rice and damp paper flowers, and head back home along the side streets, keeping up a patter of chat that you could almost mistake for sunshine.

STORYTELLING

In its cultural aspect, the community is an order of memories preserved consciously in instructions, songs, and stories.

—WENDELL BERRY, *Living by Words*

WE ARE THE STORIES we tell one another, the myths we live by. So much of who we are comes from the stew of plots over which those before us have argued fiercely, shaded and shaped and simply come to claim, because our days in a place deposit their own truths like minerals in our bones.

We move in a river of talk. Sometimes we call it gossip, sometimes policy, depending on the mood and the setting. It is both, of course. And more. It is incident, parable, the base medium of our human enterprise. The day we grow silent, the day we all agree—or cease caring enough to disagree—is the day the word will have lost its power and the beginning of all the illiteracies that afflict so many in so many places—the illiteracy of place, of the agora, of the past, and finally of the word itself. Once we have ceased to use words to any genuine purpose—telling stories, retelling history, exploring in serious debate—in their presence, how can we be baffled by the indifference of our children?

What keeps us bound to one another is our patter, swapping the inside skinny on house breaks, closing prices, love affairs. Outsiders may view this patter as a dull fruitcake of half-truths and thirdhand lies. But to us who are wed to a place, even the smallest fillip is fodder for our common life. Beneath its seeming frivolity it serves a deeper purpose. It is our ongoing engagement with the question of who we are as a community.

Traditional communities, small towns, and rural villages have always used stories to perform this function. Stories are a community's vessels, reinforcing and preserving the ways of the group. They are powerful things, and in their darker emanations they can produce a certain insularity, a hedge against outsiders, a rationale for constrictive norms of conduct.

But J.P. is *not* a traditional community, in any sense of the word, urban or otherwise. We are a hodgepodge of races, ancestries, and tongues, an urban village of twenty-three languages in the back pocket of a big city that has many other things with which to occupy its attention than us. Change, rather than conformity, has been our constant for many years now. And in such a shifting and unstable place, we have adapted the traditional function of stories to a different purpose altogether. As our one common denominator, it is they that have enabled us to grow. In sharing them, we have challenged one another and inspired one another to forge a new sort of place in the American landscape: an urban community that is genuinely diverse, culturally authentic, and publicly engaged.

We hear from one another in a countless variety of settings: while jogging around the pond, buying a set of wrenches, or stalling at the bus stop, at crime watch meetings, church coffees, garden planning sessions. Shop owners, artists, priests,

and stay-at-home moms all add to the uncommon richness of
our most common days. Dominicans, Puerto Ricans, Hondurans, Colombians, progressives, conservatives, Catholics, athe-
ists, Jews, our stories work in two ways. First, they liberate us
from stereotype. Among "our own," our stories authenticate us,
and the authority of our beingness, against the grinding ho-
mogenization of mass culture. They are the raw matter of a
shared past, customs, and dreams.

They also spring us into our individuality. For the truth is
that no two of our stories are alike, and none are simple. The
black child adopted by a progressive white couple in the seventies in Boston cannot possibly have the same story as that of
the dark-skinned Puerto Rican from Miami whose mother is
Cuban, though they've lived side by side nearly all their lives
(and bureaucracies will lump them into the same cubbyhole).
As we acknowledge the common narratives, we discover within
them a spectrum of distinctions. In a place more rooted in
storytelling than in social dogma, we are thereby given the
power to speak as individuals.

Otherwise, there are few givens, few workable cultural or
political assumptions that add up to much that is useful. Our
stories provide us with what *is* useful: the raw material for relationship. Over time they have led to our own civic narrative.
What we tell ourselves in this small urban place is that creative
civic life is possible among people of eclectic backgrounds, between rich and poor, educated and illiterate, professional and
unskilled, Latino, black, and white, those who are mobile and
those who aren't. We tell ourselves that our community
"works" on many levels, that it is a good place to live.

And the telling takes us further collectively than does the

mere experience of it. The telling amounts to the articulation of a common ideal, a structure within which we can engage the anomalies of urban existence in ways that aren't possible where people have fallen mute among one another because of stagnation or entropy. Our stories inspire us, guide us, educate us, and keep us clear. And they come about—if they come at all —in the river of talk that takes place in public.

Every place has its notable purveyors of tales, individuals who occupy a special status: part conscience, part wag. We have a stew of seasoned bards, not least our historian Michael Reiskind, and Doyle's Burke brothers.

But there is one among us who is the undisputed keeper of our stories, who attempts to see us whole and keep us honest. She is the one who is constantly stepping out into the depths to bring us back a sounding, a sense of our evolving truths. This is not a task to be undertaken lightly in a small place, least of all in a place that is as heterogeneous and contentious as ours.

Down a side street near the Monument, Sandy Storey paces a soiled rug, pours a cup of coffee from her battered blue thermos, and thinks about a cigarette. It's ten in the morning, and she's been up since six. Already she's been down to the local hospital and learned that it is closing a wing. Her mind is working now as she walks, thinking of all the organizations in town that need, desperately need, an accessible meeting place; thinking of how she'll spread the news.

Sandy's weathered almost everything there is to weather in her time by the river. A kind of earth-mother wizard with the grit of a seasoned angler, she smokes like a chimney and has the gravel-raked voice to go with it. Yet there is actually something a bit dreamy about Sandy when she is caught in mid-thought. Beneath her rose-red and gold-white curls, her blue eyes are not wholly with you, not because they are roving but because they have a curious quality of focus that, as it softens, seems to take in the emergent shape of her beloved and well-known world.

She's also a woman who likes a good laugh, and this is a good thing. It's probably what saves her sanity in a place that has the usual fare of suicides, petty lawsuits, graft, and vengeance. Now she crushes her cigarette, and the work of being a small-town weekly newspaper editor begins. There is a phone call about the rates. A weekly staff meeting with her two reporters.

This morning there's good news. The paper has won a libel defense and a slap suit against a landlord who was letting his building be used as a drug house. The summer teen program in the projects has gotten funding.

There is some not necessarily good news. Several major buildings in town have gone on the block. "I'm knee-deep in development muck," she sighs. "And I can tell you, there's a lot of testosterone poisoning out there."

And as ever, there is some reason to laugh. The wife of one of their best sources has called again. She is a doomed one-woman crusade to keep her husband's local friends. "I know he says he's on the record," she pleads once again. "But don't *let* him do it!"

And soon both the morning and the coffee are gone.

Her hair is even more unkempt by now. She is wearing a crimson sweater over a pink shirt. No makeup, no jewelry. Only in motion does it sink in: in her disregard for appearances,

Sandy is trying to make herself transparent, to encounter her world without artifice or statement; to be at home everywhere.

I offer to take her to Today's Bread or the new Thai place for lunch, and she opts instead for Brigham's, where the atmosphere is cleaner somehow, more rinsed with basic candor than those places that take your plastic. Coffee, for starters. And then some kind of sandwich. With lots of salt.

Twenty-five years ago Sandra Storey appeared in Jamaica Plain fresh from Thailand and four years in the Peace Corps. Born and raised in Ohio, she still bore the Midwest in her twang and her bearing. Candid, earnest, and down-home, she came with a three-month-old daughter and a head filled with poetry. She took up residence in the Brookside neighborhood just outside Egleston Square. She wrote, picked up teaching jobs where she could, and in her spare time volunteered for various causes, from Greenpeace to the fledgling local chapter of the National Writers' Union.

Activism had been a byword around her family dinner table back home in a small town outside Dayton, Ohio, and she wasn't about to change her ways—and probably couldn't have even if she'd wanted to. "My parents were always involved locally," she recalls. "Always had a lot of opinions and conversations, at the dinner table, about public policy."

She worked for McCarthy and then for Kennedy during the '68 campaign. In Bangkok she'd rallied against Spiro Agnew.

"By the time I was twenty-six, I thought of myself as a writer who was always getting dragged into politics." She grins as she picks at her french fries. "I didn't want to be working on these issues. But you just had to, because they were there. It's a gravitational force." She shrugs. "I just can't help it."

Jamaica Plain in '73 was a magnetic force field for a woman of Sandy's proclivities. Its identity as a thriving white middle-class Main Street town was being rent by the birth of something quite other—something that looked, at that historic moment at any rate, a lot like death. The old patterns and civilities, the old ways and stories, were coming to an end. Among the elderly there was a feeling of grief, wounded pride, and betrayal. In their wake, arriving poor Puerto Rican families and blacks in Bromley-Heath were frustrated, demanding greater political franchise, better education for their kids, and a sense of ownership in the place they were inheriting. She and the young whites who'd come after her were just another part of the town's changing picture. It was the grist of poetry, this tale of death and birth, growth and change. But instead of toiling at her desk, she found herself out in the streets. And there, she experienced an epiphany.

"I was driving around town, doing my errands, and being drawn by this strange feeling. I remember thinking, 'I just *love* this town.' I'd never felt that about a geographical location before. You know?"

I do, but at the moment I'm far more interested in how this message sat with Sandy in the early seventies. The answer is: it didn't. It burbled and boiled and eventually burst on her that she didn't want to dabble anymore. She wanted to get in, up to her elbows, up to her soul. She didn't want to work away in the realm of metaphor and symbol; she wanted to have a hand in creating what J.P. needed, an articulated and sustainable vision of itself into which every segment of a rapidly changing place would be woven.

Soon after this, at a party, she met a member of the newly formed Neighborhood Development Corporation. The conversation turned to economic development. She learned that the group was planning to take over the abandoned brewery near her home and generate new businesses there.

The brewery was an eyesore and a hazard. She knew of a few artists who squatted in loft space there. But other than that, she and the neighbors regarded it as Brookside's white elephant. When asked if she'd be willing to host a coffee for her neighbors so that the NDC could describe what they were trying to do with the project, she readily agreed.

But coffees were small potatoes. Each day as she walked her daughter in the neighborhood, she became more and more aware of the absence of playgrounds, the abandoned properties, the general destitution, and the incredible opportunity that lay around her.

She wasn't alone. By now handfuls of small and disparate groups had come to life to tackle one problem or another. All of them were well intentioned, but they were a disorganized lot, and even the very best work they did alone wouldn't result in any greater overall coherence in the neighborhood, unless they began to talk to one another.

In the winter of 1984, they did. A group of eighteen organizations agreed to work together for as long as it took to arrive at an accurate picture of what Jamaica Plain needed—in housing, parks, transportation—and create a coherent plan for their subsequent efforts.

Sandy became one of the more than one hundred participants. The Jamaica Plain Community Planning Coalition met every single Wednesday evening for a year and a half. In September 1985 it presented its report to the community. Its vision called for disposing of vacant and abandoned properties, shared public zoning oversight, improved sanitation, and increased funding for public spaces, outdoor sitting areas where residents could congregate and socialize. "A Plan for Jamaica Plain" was to become the community's working paper, part dream, part blueprint.

Sometimes timing is everything; it certainly was for Jamaica Plain in the mid-eighties. A newly elected mayor gave the city's neighborhoods significant advisory powers over housing, development, and zoning issues in local neighborhood councils. And members of the Jamaica Plain Community Planning Coalition stood ready.

Sandy was among the first to be nominated to the Jamaica Plain Neighborhood Council. And before she knew what was happening, the council chose her to be its first chair. But if her poetry had disappeared, her sense of the worth of stories hadn't. In the course of things, she'd met several local mothers like herself, who were concerned with pushing an agenda of social change that would strengthen and preserve the fabric of their community rather than tear it apart.

These were hardly abstract questions. Each day these women made choices about neighborhood development, poor people's housing, and the delivery of food to the hungry that dramatically affected the quality of their private worlds. Their own lives had become the stories they needed to tell one another, in order to continue to live them, day after day, with integrity.

What began as casual camaraderie, the occasional phone call after the kids were in bed, became a story circle. They talked at night over their kitchen tables about the lives they would resume the next morning. For the first time, Sandy experienced the power of words used as an amalgam of the personal and the public, of desire and hard-nosed analysis; stories that had some enduring public grain, shared among those with a common public goal.

"Mostly we told anecdotes," she recalls. " 'Oh, you won't believe what happened.' Or 'I said to so-and-so, "I really hope you support this bill." ' Or 'I swear to God someone tried to trip me on the stairs.' " But in time their purpose became more serious: to share their stories in order to help women like themselves who were trying to make a difference at the grassroots level, in their own communities.

The result was *Women in Citizen Advocacy*, a book published in 1991, which Sandy co-authored with Georgia Mattison. *Women in Citizen Advocacy* is a community activists' how-to, full of stories of successful women, concrete tips about the political process, and advice about avoiding some of the pitfalls and becoming as effective as possible. It features stories of women who've done groundbreaking work in drug-rehab programs for mothers; run successful campaigns for mass transit; and gotten anti-dumping legislation passed and clothing allowances for children on welfare.

In the years since Sandy first arrived, Jamaica Plain had transformed itself. It was a more stable community, more settled into its identity as an interesting, hands-on kind of place, largely thanks to the work of people like herself, Winky, Slug, Femke, and Ruth Parker. And she possessed a store of wisdom that twelve years of hard work had won. She'd observed what worked and what didn't, who stayed and who didn't. And she understood, in a way she hadn't at the start, the incredibly gradual, organic nature of community growth.

Sandy had just turned forty, and she wanted to stand in the deeper passes, to cast her line in just the right spots and return to tell what she'd seen of the conditions.

That year she resigned from the J.P. Neighborhood Council and took a job as a newspaper reporter.

We've been talking for more than an hour. Now she leans across the Formica counter and squints. "Is your tape recorder on?" She laughs, a chorus of hasps. "I ask as one who has made that mistake more than I care to remember."

The Jamaica Plain Citizen, forty years old, was published weekly, part of a modest chain that included the neighboring towns of Hyde Park and Dorchester. As a result, it didn't depend entirely for its profits on its scrupulous coverage of a single polity. From a business viewpoint, this was sensible (indispensable, some would say); but from the community's, it was less so.

As on many small-town papers, the staff of the *Citizen* was overworked. Editors relied on community press releases for much of their copy. The town regarded the *Citizen* with the fondness it might have for its passable high school football team. The paper did what it did well—school notes, club announcements, recent marriages and promotions, a chatty astrology column, and homey reminders like "Mother's Day Is This Sunday"—and it caused no waves.

Within the constraints of being the sole source for local news in town, Sandy learned the ropes. She covered local meetings, kept a low profile, and rose rapidly. From 1986 to 1990 she went from editorial assistant to editor in chief. She was focused in a way most town reporters are not who use their first reporting stints as stepping stones. Sandy wasn't going anywhere. This was her life's work. She was the chronicler of her particular place.

She began to agitate for improvements. She wanted more staffers, and she wanted them better paid. She initiated a unionization effort among the editorial staff of ten. Wages improved, but working conditions deteriorated. Her staff became demoralized over petty personnel politics and the owners' unwillingness to invest more in the paper's editorial operation. In the summer of 1991, discouraged and with no prospects of other work, Sandy quit. The community deserved better, and so did she.

A recent divorce had left her with a small bit of capital.

"Was the community clamoring for me?" she says. "No. Was anyone saying, 'We really need you'? I don't think so. I had three thousand dollars, and I thought it would be really cool to put my money where my mouth was and see if I really could make a good paper work."

In February 1991 the first issue of *The Jamaica Plain Gazette* hit the streets. In two bold strokes Sandy thumbed her nose at the time-honored tradition of subscription weeklies. She made her tabloid free and circulated it to every home in town. When residents picked it up that day, they were in for another surprise: J.P.'s second newspaper was bilingual. And nothing in town has really been the same since.

Every working day Sandy leaves her house at nine-thirty and drives the half-dozen blocks to her office in the rear basement of a converted family home just off Centre, beneath her land- lord, Stavros Frantzis. She checks her messages, mobilizes her staff, picks up the phone. A carafe of fake pink daisies anchors a stack of past issues. An old shoebox, transformed into the semblance of a mailbox, hangs on the wall by the door. The clutter of long-past deadlines and the markings of life amid the confetti of breaking news lend the office much the same atmosphere as Sandy herself.

Sandy is still earnest, still down-home. But now, as an editor and publisher, she is canny as well. Her philosophy, if it can be reduced to anything so simple, is that a community paper, if it's worth anything, has to be accessible, credible, and accountable—accountable not to some set of abstract big-media norms, but to the terms of the community's life.

"Typically what happens, particularly in urban neighbor-hoods, is that no matter what paper you do, no matter what circulation, there will be fifty to one hundred community ac-tivists who read it," she says. "It's the other people who are up for grabs. The more disenfranchised people really don't know a local paper exists. So they and other disenfranchised types, like newcomers, don't even know what to complain about or how to do it. It seemed obvious, first of all, to do a tabloid, second to put Spanish in it, and third to make it total market saturation."

Community response was immediate. "We had lots of people in the minority community, and lots of young people, between

I'd say twenty and thirty-five, saying, 'Oh, thank goodness, J.P. finally has a newspaper!' Which is just what I thought: they hadn't even known there *was* one before. But boy, you put it on their front walk . . . and . . . the degree of participation and ownership people begin to feel in the community is amazing."

Part of what readers have responded to is the seriousness of the effort. Every issue brings us news of the many meetings we can't attend and of important discussions taking place between local interests and city agencies. We read about developers turning artists' studios into condos, after-school youth programs for at-risk teens, gang mediation efforts, and improvements in the neighborhood schools. Businesses come and go on its pages, as does the evergreen problem of public transportation on our increasingly congested main streets. And without fail we can turn to the weekly police reports, real estate closing prices, events calendar, history column, and letters page.

"It's my job to reflect the community back to itself as best as possible," Sandy says as we stand up. "To keep people informed." She stops and peruses the pavement, then says thoughtfully, "It sounds so simple and unsophisticated, but it isn't."

Indeed, the stakes of credibility for a small-town paper are as high as, if not higher than, those of major city media. Accuracy is essential. There's no forgiving a misnamed child, a mishandled quote, or misidentified family pet in small-town news. But if details count for much in the reliability of local copy, *which* details are deemed newsworthy makes up the balance of readers' enduring confidence. Most everyone around town knows the dirt. They can tell you about money laundering, or where the illegal gaming goes on in the basements of Hyde Square, and who is sleeping with whom. But Sandy would never print any of it just for publishing's sake. There is no profit, in small towns, in airing the laundry simply for effect, as Sandy is the first to tell you. So much of our lives is played out and acted out in public, in our arts, social and civic involvement, churchgoing, and support groups. Perhaps we don't need the salacious details to satisfy our need for meaningful connection; perhaps our exposure to one another has a humbling effect on the perilous human tendency toward self-righteousness.

Sandy seems to understand instinctively that we don't need our public record to tell us what we already know. We need it to perform a higher function that we *cannot* perform as individuals—gossips *or* citizens. News here, to be news, must be relevant to the functioning life of the place, to our sense of polity. It is in many ways the subtlest and most demanding aspect of her work. On the quality of Sandy's news judgment rests the paper's reliability. There can't be many off days.

We've settled back into the office. Behind Sandy, the computer blips messages continually. "There are the hundred community activists here who want to drive the news," Sandy says. "And that's fine; that's their job. But we need to keep a wider view. I'm always thinking about trends and people and things we have a problem getting a handle on. I worry: is the particular truth we've carved out about J.P. so far, is our version anywhere close to right?

"It's good not to be daily sometimes," she muses. "I hate snapshot journalism, which is what I call a lot of the daily hardnews coverage. I'd be so scared if I was one of those reporters.

You take that snapshot and hope it was the right piece of reality, that it will hold up tomorrow.

"Here we have time to talk to all the parties and piece together what happened in a controversy. I don't know if other community newspapers have this, but my motto is, 'If it doesn't seem quite right, if we haven't got it yet—well, it doesn't go into this issue. It goes into the next one.' "

Part of "getting it right" entails ensuring that the paper remains a genuinely open forum. "People are pretty open," Sandy says. "Only on rare occasions do they try to go off the record or refuse to talk. It's part of the uniqueness of J.P. Sometimes they try to be secretive with me." She gets a gleam in her eye. "I give them a little bit of leeway, but then I say, 'Okay, come clean. You're a community organization.' And bless their hearts, they figure out a way."

Part of getting it right is achieving balance, writing about the entire spectrum of community concerns, and from time to time ruffling feathers for a good cause. The *Gazette* publishes all the stories we don't want to know, that vex our satisfaction and try our hope that good will follow on good, that the revitalization of a place ought not to hurt as it heals. But they are the stories that, if we are thinking people at all, force us to examine the deeper complexities of what it is to live in a place that doesn't exist purely at the disposition of a continuous tradition, but rather has its being in the rapids of change.

The shootings, the drug trafficking, the displacement of poor people—these stories, too, are Sandy's responsibility. They may be her chief responsibility, the place where credibility verges into accountability. The unspoken contract between a local editor and her audience involves not just the way in which morsels of information are handled but the larger context of understanding as well.

At the end of a nine-hour workday, Sandy goes home to have dinner. Then commences the evening shift. "I've got two briefcases. One's for news, the other's for business. You see, I'm not only the editor, I'm the publisher, too. I do all the payroll, I pay all the bills, I do all the bookkeeping, the spreadsheets, the budget. I have to figure out the rates and work on sales campaign materials.

"Let's see, what did I do Thursday night? I edited copy. I planned the stories for the Mission Hill edition. I did one last look over the photo shoots for both papers over the weekend. I typed an ad. And I wrote a memo after a meeting with somebody about an ad-share agreement."

Finally she turned to her stack of minutes from meetings of the week. "People know we can't go to every meeting, but they also know we're not going to blow them off." She reads assiduously. When she sees something important, she picks up the phone and makes a call. "Like, residents were looking for trash cans on Washington Street, and they weren't coming and they weren't coming. So I said, 'Well, time for a little media coverage of the trash cans.' "

Treating people with respect, being accountable, has built Sandy's capital as keeper of our tales. Ads have consistently increased, and so have the number of pages. But most important to Sandy, so have her phone calls.

"The beauty of J.P. is that it's an incredibly wonderful two-way street here, doing the news," she says with deflective modesty. "Lots of people are constantly feeding me ideas. I talked about the 'one hundred' activists. Fortunately, in J.P. today there are six hundred. Other people do it, too. They just dial that number."

When she attends meetings or hearings downtown, she says now with a rare show of pride, she can tell immediately if the citizens come from a town with a good local paper or not. "There's almost a symbiosis between having a paper and the degree to which a neighborhood is empowered," she says. "When we started a Mission Hill edition, there was literally no events or meeting calendar. Now they have a neighborhood organization, a trade council, and more—and all of them are starting to hold the city and each other accountable for everything from potholes to crime."

But there is something worse than conflict, Sandy knows. And that is satisfaction. "One thing we have to keep our eyes on is not to become complacent about how wonderful we are," she says. "I learned that lesson working in Cambridge for a while. They got to a point where they couldn't say there was a racial tension problem somewhere because 'we don't have racial tension problems in Cambridge.'

"I pray to God that never happens in Jamaica Plain. Denial. I watch it like a hawk. With a tolerant community, that can be very subtle.

"Take community policing. A family on Goldsmith Street over on Pondside called to say they were really upset because a hobo was going through their trash. They called the police and nobody came. And a woman called from Egleston Square and said she was really upset because every night a guy beat up his wife in front of her window, and she called the police and nobody came. Talk about contrasting realities."

She pauses. "The one thing they had in common was that nobody came!" She laughs. "In my neighborhood the guys go through the trash all the time to get the bottles and cans. It would never occur to us to call the police."

We used to argue more, she says ruefully. Didn't matter what the meeting was about, it would invariably attract at least forty residents, all of them in a fighting mood. Small-town process vigilantes, fierce in staking their claims to genuine representative community in what seemed at the time the dusk of local democracy.

Today, meetings are quieter, more orderly. We are a more organized, established polity. Consensus and compromise come more easily. The factions are more predictably drawn. Fewer candidates run opposed.

Part of this is having a newspaper that informs us and acts as a forum for our many voices. But let it not be said that people can't always find something to disagree about in J.P.

Sandy's fiftieth birthday coincided with the fifth anniversary of *The Gazette*, and two hundred friends decided to throw a surprise party.

"They held meetings beforehand at Doyle's." She laughs. "*Lots* of meetings. I've never seen such a community effort. Of course, everybody argued about how to do it. Finally, they decided they'd hold a bash at the firehouse. I was taken out for dinner, and afterward my friend who teaches art asked if I would help him carry some big bags of clay, which were at the firehouse, out to his car. Of course I believed him!

"When I walked in, the place was dark. Suddenly, I heard the theme from *2001*. A hundred and fifty flashlights flipped on. The mayor sent a proclamation. Doyle's sent over free food. There was music. It was great."

We learn from the past and from one another, and this is why a paper is so essential. A good community paper is like a moving portrait. It maintains the present-day dialogue, keeps us focused on what is outside our small narcissistic concerns. It gives us a chance to be politically grown up in a society where we are constantly bombarded by infantilism, to eschew the happy-ever-after endings. And to know that there is more listening and more telling to do, more stories to hear, even as the last page is turned on the written word.

LEAVING

IT IS SHORTLY AFTER DINNER on one of those evenings that spell a lull between summer and the crispness of fall, and I am taking my two-year-old on a walk down our street before his bath. The squirrels are busy. I find object lessons dropped from great heights in the oaks, profligate lessons. He is pleased to sit in his stroller and learn: here is a green chestnut; here the teeth marks of the prudent hoarder overhead. It is a sweet hour that needs no other company, but just now we hear a front door swing open, and Tracy is standing there inviting us in to play with Ben.

For two years doors have continuously opened like this on the street. But now, as my toddler moves gleefully toward the familiar toys, Tracy sinks into the sofa in a fresh bout of tears. They are moving, to neighboring Newton. Tracy, her husband, and Ben are the fourth defection on the street in less than a year, and all but one have left for the same reason: the schools.

I've lived here long enough to see two generations of young

talented professionals with an interest in public urban life move out for the same reason. But now that I am a mother, these moves touch me much closer to home. With each departure I see another rent in the fabric of love and familiarity, and with it all that my son has learned about the world outside his home. Tracy is crying because Ben's first friendships, his first world of discovery, and beauty, and skinned knees, will be left behind. And a great deal of luck besides.

It takes enormous work and a load of chance to make community in this nomadic culture of ours. The people in this town have a knack for it. And she knows too well that there's no guarantee that the neighbors in the more affluent suburb they are moving to, with its superior schools and services, will be as good at it—or even feel the need for it. Reports from those who've preceded her aren't terribly encouraging. People in the suburbs aren't as public with one another as we are. They're less likely to run across the street to cut into a fresh-baked pie, or sit on the front stoop waiting for the fireflies to come out.

But Tracy and her husband have done the arithmetic: to remain in the city with two children would cost them thirty thousand dollars a year in private tuition—not counting any extras—and these, unlike higher mortgages, aren't deductible.

Tonight as I watch her mourn, I wonder what we are saying about ourselves as a culture that such a terrible choice must be made by educated and prosperous adults who for every other reason would dearly love to remain in a place that has so enriched them with affection and the opportunity to learn to live in community. Like those before them, they are under no illusions about the price they are paying for decent education. They will give up serious engagement with the city and its social issues. They will find themselves in more homogeneous settings with nice enough people who have traded stimulation for comfort. They will see few black faces and hear no Spanish, except from the poor women who come in each morning to clean. And they fear deep down that they will be cheating their children of authentic culture by offering them a sanitized version of it—safe, uncontroversial, and, as their children reach the age of independence, claustrophobic towns, with their idyllic boutiques and border strip malls and little else in between, except, of course, the schools.

But most of all Tracy is grieving the loss of community, and with it the possibility of a very specific kind of education that is virtually nonexistent in the American urban experience today. Learning once was integral to life on the street, with its shared projects and meals and parental roles among neighbors who'd become as close as kin. Skills were passed on to one's familiars. As learning advanced, it took in a broader cut of the world, deepened a child's comprehension of numerous relationships and truths, his own among them, and in turn expected ever greater accountability and competence from him, both intellectual and ethical. And so it went, into his productive years. The world of the village was filled by neighbors who, among their many other roles, were always teachers and learners.

Soon I too will stand at this crossroads. The lengths to which parents before me have gone to remain in the community without spending exorbitant sums on private schools are heroic. A couple of friends, realizing they could no longer afford private school for their daughters, enrolled them in one of the city's charter schools. These are publicly financed schools free of union requirements. There are four charter schools in Boston, and each offers an innovative curriculum. Now the girls travel downtown each morning, and their mother spends several lunch hours each week with them at the school. The father gets home early so that he can spend with them the four hours a night he says are necessary to augment classroom instruction.

One group of Jamaica Plain parents went even further. They designed a charter school for Jamaica Plain, a "neighborhood" elementary that would have used our abundant greenspace and zoo as the basis for a nature curriculum. But the proposal didn't pass the stiff competitive process, and many of its proponents have since left town for the suburbs.

Among the families that remain of my son's original neighborhood playmates, we are the only one willing to give the public schools a look. The Agassiz Elementary School has been recommended by my friend Sue on the city's school committee. It is one of the newer elementaries in the system, built in the early seventies as a combination school–community center. The notion is impressive and quite old-fashioned: learning ought to be a lifelong and publicly supported affair. But these days the "community center" functions mostly as a gym facility for kids and a meeting space for community organizations, at night and on weekends. The school runs just like every other school in the system, beginning with the first bell at nine-twenty.

I arrive early to look around. It's not a bad building, as modern schools go. Its concrete is broken here and there by bright blue and red patches, decorative plates in the windows. Even the white paint that temporarily masks the graffiti has a bold and attentive character to it.

The problem is, I can't find the front door. I drive past what looks like a loading dock, with a sign posted on it that reads: STAFF PARKING ONLY. There are no windowed entryways, no obvious foyers or reception halls. The entrance to the modern school is a supreme exercise in architectural camouflage. And I decide as I sit in my car, trying to deconstruct the physical intentions of the place, that this is not a propitious way to begin if you are a school.

By eight-ten this morning, children are beginning to arrive. School buses tool around the neighborhood, picking up those to be bused hither and yon. But these early birds arrive on foot or by car, dropped off by parents on their way to work. Mostly they are black. In the large playing field out behind the school, people are still exercising their dogs and jogging the perimeter. An Asian boy peddles a red tricycle that's too small for him, then shoulders it on his back and walks away.

I am mindful, as I watch this scene, of two of the inalterable facts about the choice of middle-class white parents to remain in an urban school system. The first is the increasing isolation that my son will experience in his own neighborhood, where middle-class parents of all races move out, as Tracy is doing, once the school years begin. And the second is racial isolation: he'll be one of the few, if not the only, white boy in his class. On the face of it, this wouldn't be cause for concern, were it not for an offhand remark made by his baby-sitter a while back.

"Are you going to send him to public school?" she asked one day. A lanky blonde with superb basketball skills, she has made her way through the system to Boston Latin, the prestigious exam school.

"I'm not sure," I answered truthfully.

"Well, he'll have a much harder time of it than I did," she said matter-of-factly. "Not only is he white, he's a boy."

This exchange, I admit, chills me as I follow another parent in through what I've finally decided is the door.

To make this choice will mean hard work. Lots of it. It will mean aggressively lobbying for the good teachers, and making sure, like my friend who spends her lunches at school, that I can be on top of what's going on.

When I'd called to make an appointment two weeks ago, the phone rang in some office inside this fortress twenty times without being answered. I rang up again, immediately. This time someone in that office actually picked up the receiver and hung up on me without a word. I rang again, and the phone went unanswered. I counted twenty rings.

I can't imagine needing to find my child and being unable to get through. The parents I know who've remained with the public schools work so hard in them that their kids' education becomes a second career. They have learned to keep an eye on things by being useful. They volunteer to tutor in their children's classes, ferry groups from place to place, serve on parents' councils, run special projects.

When I finally got through the switchboard the next morning promptly at eight, a man's voice answered. I was somewhat mollified. He was genial. Witty. It turned out that he was the principal. He invited me to come by the next day, or the day after. He'd be happy to show me around.

So this was how it worked, I thought as I put down the phone. Parents who remain active enter into league with the pockets of excellence that exist in a baggy and not terribly accountable system. Together they work, against and around—

and where they must, with—the protected forces of mediocrity and inertia.

The foyer is large and open, with mazes of up and down ramps and crossways, quilts and banners and announcement boards. I find the office without difficulty and am handed over to a Ms. R. Formerly principal at another elementary school in town, Ms. R. is a compact woman who has the commanding step of a vanishing breed. She is ending her long and satisfying career as vice principal here. She is an old hand and proud of her institution.

There are nine hundred students here, she confirms as we walk. Big, yes.

But—she breaks stride—there's always a waiting list, you know. We are moving down a hallway that's been splashed with a bright orange. The kindergarten wing is just ahead. Now she stops us again, finger raised. K1 (nursery) is about to be phased out. She peers at me. I will, of course, understand. The mayor wants all K children to have an extended day. That's a priority. I nod.

We pass through heavy orange doors designed to maintain a secluded and calm ambience for the school's youngest pupils. There are four classrooms here, two bilingual and two English speaking. I've visited many pre-school classes by now, and these are no different in any dramatic particulars from the most privileged. The cupboards and shelves are full of books and activities, the walls with art, and the easels with works in progress. The teachers, with the exception of one, are engaged—reading, guiding activities, or preparing the children for rest time. They are gentle, and the children seem happy in their presence.

Before the hour is out, I will understand in a way that I

couldn't before I spent time here, just how high the trade-offs are when parents like me opt out of the experience of diversity in favor of the homogeneous and familiar. If my son were to come to school here, he would meet children from all over the world and encounter an array of differences that he would learn to understand, accommodate, and accept. He would learn Spanish at a younger age than he would in any other kind of school, and he would have it constantly reinforced by the conversation of his peers. His art classes would be taught by painters, dancers, and musicians from the community. He'd meet Bosnian children and visually impaired kids who learn in a specially equipped classroom; pre-schoolers in need of the enrichments he's been lucky enough to have received; and women on welfare who are learning how to be classroom aides in order to move out of poverty and system dependence. There are lessons that can't be learned, or learned well, unless a child experiences them in the daily context of their own lived truth. In a society so deeply divided along class lines, these are the experiences that a public school in a place like J.P. can offer its young.

I ask if I can return and sit in on a first-grade class, then I leave by way of the playing field out back.

It is swarming with activity on this late spring day. The fifth-graders are running an all-school Olympics that, I was informed, they've been planning for weeks. At varying points around the field, children sit at card tables and hand out passes. The younger ones are throwing themselves into the spirit of the event with abandon.

It is not at all unlike a private school fair I attended with my son several weeks earlier. That morning children could choose from among pony rides and giant inflatable slides, face painting, and a midway with prizes from ball launchers to teddy bears. Now I watch the children of the city. They roll tires and jump rope and kick worn-out balls. They laugh over hula hoops and vie for position in the Chinese–jump rope contest. And I see with a greater clarity than ever before how alike children are in their desire to stretch body and mind and soul to the limits of what is possible. And why we must remain passionate about what it means to give them—all of them—our best.

It is for this that I return the next Friday. Because in the end, school isn't just a context for socialization but a place where children learn. I haven't forgotten that, as good as social impressions are, the Boston schools' record of achievement scores is fairly abysmal. From fourth grade through high school, the percentage of functional illiterates increases from 25 to an astounding 80 percent (based on the Stanford 9 test criteria: "little or no mastery of knowledge and skills needed for satisfactory work").

This time when I arrive, the principal, Mr. Nunez, is behind closed doors with a discipline matter. I stand in the office for ten minutes. Five adult members of the staff wander in and out. They look at me, then past me, without a word. Finally I decide to track down the unflappable Ms. R.

I find her in the Xerox room cursing at a stubborn machine. After several minutes, during which time I simply witness her irritation at an object that like myself refuses to budge, she apparently concludes that of the two, I am the more easily disposed of. She strides to the intercom system that connects the office to each room and dials. Can a prospective mother come up and sit in on Mrs. T.'s class? Will she send someone down to take me up?

It is settled, and Ms. R. can return to her other annoyance. I wait by the counter looking toward the door and all at once find myself staring at a young Hispanic boy who is being dragged into the office on the arms of two aging, overweight white men. No more than nine, the boy is shaking with rage, his fists ready to strike the first object they can. I take a step back.

"No!" His voice is trembling, low and harsh. "I don't want to go!"

Inside the office the men drop him from their arms. No one in the office receives him or even acknowledges his presence. The men, having discharged their duty, roam around the office; the boy, Thomas, also roams. The adversaries circle each other among the clutter of metal desks like two orbits gone awry. The boy is robotic, cornered, out of control. He stalks and swears.

"You kicked me!" he accuses one of the men.

"Okay, Thomas, if that's how you feel." The men taunt him. "I'm sorry, Thomas."

At wit's end, Thomas careens around the counter and shoves boxes of loose papers onto the floor.

"Motherfuckers!" he screams.

The men turn, chuckling, and amble out into the hall.

The boy continues to pace, a wounded animal. Then he is suddenly quiet. From the door where I've taken up my position again, I can feel a dark energy in him, drawing him inward and gathering strength. Something is about to happen.

Thomas comes toward me. He has found a rock and is hiding it beneath his coat. What is a rock like this doing in a school office?

I'm asking myself this, when I hear Thomas call out to the two men, then hear the sound of the rock as it is hurled, and skitters, and comes to a stop on the linoleum floor.

"That's it!" I hear one of the fat men yell. "Thomas just assaulted me with a rock! Call the school police!"

Just now the two little girls who are to lead me to their class appear. I hurry them off, in an effort to protect them from what is about to happen. But I'm shaken. All my certainties of the week before have been blown away, as I consider Thomas, his life and its terrible dark holes, and the destructive force such children have on a school and the children around them, like the two who are proudly marching me upstairs.

The scene in Mrs. T.'s classroom is weary. The Easter artwork is still up—regulation-issue bunnies and xeroxed floral baskets the children have colored in. Mrs. T. is alone with twenty children today. The average class size is twenty-eight, but come May there is the natural attrition of those families less committed to the endeavor.

Mrs. T. is trying to lead a small round-table book discussion with three of the children. The rest are seated at desks arranged in a large rectangle facing inward, filling in spelling worksheets. Most have finished or have decided not to do them. They lean on their desks, or run up to the blackboard and play with the chalk, or read one another's answers, or torment one another.

Behind them on the blackboard is a large handwritten spelling exercise. Perhaps it is the lesson for the day. I copy it down, I find its message such a curious choice for six-year-olds:

My Cat

My cat is a bad cat. When I touch her, she scratches me. When I run, she chases me. When I eat, she knocks my food down, and I whoop [sic] her. Then she bites me.

I am sure that there is good pedagogical reasoning behind using a reading method that involves children in small-group work. I am just as sure that the rest of the children are simply wasting their time.

Mrs. T. seems to understand this, too. She is seasoned and wise and attempts with some success to control the disorder in the rectangle as she nudges along a discussion with her group about the activities of sea creatures. I'd like to think that on other days she has an aide to oversee the three-quarters of the students that are now either dozing or randomly trying to entertain one another.

But now a teacher from the other half of this "open" classroom interrupts my thoughts. She lets loose a brutal scream that halts all action in our quadrant.

"Get over here! Put that down this minute!"

The girls at the rectangle freeze. They snap around to look at me. Will I be shocked? Or will I, like the steady and ultimately helpless Mrs. T., pretend I've heard nothing of this uncontrolled outburst and simply bend back over my book?

I return their glance with sympathy. But my attention (like

theirs) has shifted to the action next door. An adult voice has begun to read in a droning monotone.

"There are eighty-seven kinds of whales, dolphins, and porpoises . . . Whales, dolphins, and porpoises . . ." Soon even I begin to lose the thread.

I stand up and sidle over to where I can see what's going on. The children in this class are lined up in four rows of desks facing the blackboard. It is journal time. The screamer is standing at the board. Now she pauses in her narrative to draw a large circle. The children obediently copy her in their journals. She writes WHALE in the center of her circle. The children do the same. Next, she draws a branch out to the right.

"See?" she points to a large picture in the book. "This is the *right* whale. Write RIGHT here."

The children obey. The teacher draws another branch below this one.

"Now," she says, "write BLUE here." The children obey.

I find myself putting on my apologist's cap. After all, my son would probably only be here for two years before transferring to a more advanced magnet program for another one, two, or three years. And by then he'd almost be ready for exam school.

And then I stop.

I leave the Agassiz deeply discouraged. Does a school exist today that considers our social goals as communities and our intellectual goals as a civilization to be of a piece, and conveys them in this light and equally well? Both learning and communities are partly about making the "new" well and sound. To do so, they depend on each other. The past offers some, but by no means all, of the answers. To advance to new ground, we've learned in Jamaica Plain, requires conditions of order, consistency, rhythms of concentrated individual effort alternating with spirited engagement and interdependence. Learning and communities are the twin faces of culture.

But little about the contemporary school seems to be engaged in making these connections. If the ultimate purpose of education is not to equip us to live as deeply and effectively as possible in relation to self and others—to live in community—then what is it?

These days in the public schools—in my city, at any rate—children are uprooted from their neighborhoods, the source of all meaningful experience of the world beyond family, and are placed in groups of strangers. Educators talk about the importance of this group to the child's acquisition of "social skills." What they really mean is the child's development of basic ego tasks: defending and negotiating one's turf and playthings. Conforming to rules. Controlling basic impulses. Skills that are, to be sure, essential to any social order but inadequate to the challenge of community. For that challenge, children need to learn about cooperation and responsibility in a setting that models and expects this behavior from all its members.

However, on top of this arrangement has been placed another one, intended to address the differing intellectual requirements of the students, and this is the siphoning off of some students into magnet and gifted programs in other school buildings at, usually, two-year intervals, wreaking havoc on any consistent opportunity for cooperative group experience.

The alternative to this disruption, short of leaving the city, is the walk-to private school. Private schools make much of "membership." Their orientation programs at the beginning of the school year involve parents, teachers, students, and administrators in gatherings and discussions. The purpose is to move these individuals beyond casual acquaintance, for what most assume will be many years of their lives, and to focus the attention of *all* members of the "school community" on their shared endeavor. Student conduct and obligations, teachers' expectations, and the ever-important role of parents are all discussed explicitly and in detail.

Within the daily life of most private schools, community behavior is a constant and conscious pedagogical element. Everything from study habits to seating arrangements in the dining room, from the school's judicial process for breaches of norms (where students frequently participate in the decision-making process) to the volunteer activities of parents, is fodder for deepening the community's understanding of itself and the behaviors that sustain and strengthen it.

I am reminded of a conversation I had with the principal of the Agassiz school the first day I visited. He was interested in turning our discussion to the matter of public education in general, and his school in particular.

In a number of schools, he said, parents' councils have become hotbeds of activism and militance around special interests like special education and bilingual programs, a situation that sometimes benefits but often paralyzes school administrators. Yet he regretted, he told me, the absence of an active parents' council at Agassiz. Here the parents were either too overwhelmed by life's other demands to take an interest in educational policy, or they simply didn't care. The leadership stopped calling meetings because they could never get a quorum.

He was sorry about this, he said, because after twelve years as a principal and even more before that as a teacher, he knew that tunnel vision becomes a liability of the work: the showcase curriculum project, the cutting-edge technology. We need parents to help us take our blinders off, he told me. But lacking them, we do the best job we can.

He tells parents: as long as you love your child, feed and clothe him, read to him, and take him to the parks and the zoo and public cultural programs in the neighborhood, and come to our special events—assemblies and presentations—we'll do the rest.

His modest gospel gave me pause. This was precisely the division of labor and responsibility that my parents and teachers had understood when I was growing up. My parents, busy with other children and the business of earning a living, didn't hang out at my school or demand certain programs or accountability, and they certainly didn't spend their evenings locked in discussions of educational policy.

Indeed, if one thing distinguishes private schools from public—or public schools today from those of the past—it is the clear understanding that has evolved of what roles meet the needs of children at varying stages of their development; those of educators in making it happen, and those of parents in supporting them. Tradition, a sense that what worked in the past still holds value, and a refined division of labor—among policy and curriculum executives (administrators), those who convey them (teachers), and those who support them (parents)—allow these schools to maintain a very real community existence for all associated with them.

The sad irony is that while private-school students experience more community life within the confines of their institutions than public-school students under current conditions possibly can, it is the rare private school in which students have a chance to connect these skills to the "real" world. Conversely, where the "real community" comes into play in public schools, it is given no intellectual form that would advance the broader social goals on which it is based. Simply throwing kids of diverse backgrounds together without some organic and consistent discussion of community becomes in practice an exercise in random, short-term relationships.

Sadly, little of what we've done to diversify student bodies and their curricula—busing, assignment procedures, enrichment programs—has resolved the social imbalances and segregation that these solutions were meant to address. And the price has been high: the loss of community within the schools and the eroding support of them among middle-class members of the communities around them.

Moreover, little effort is made to integrate academic lessons into children's experience as members of a learning community, of the larger community outside. The "cooperative learning" method now used in some elementary and middle schools teaches children how to team up in small groups and to coach one another on the material. Sometimes it is done well. Often it is not. And community-building skills of any sort become less valued, less relevant, and less frequently applied with each successive grade of school. Off the school premises, learning is generally confined to field trips to museums and other stimulating events—a good break from the boredom of the class-room. Rarely does it involve visits to or projects with local businesses, nursing homes, or residents.

We've gotten hopelessly mired in the style instead of the substance of the issue. Friendships made in both public and private schools tend to retract into the more habitual patterns of neighborhood, class, and race once the school years are over. Our children need explicit and practical tools, a pedagogy that connects learning to the community: a community curriculum.

Our schools are our last, best recourse for teaching us what we most need to know: how to live together, to envision the kind of community life we want, to discipline ourselves within it, to experience abundance in the midst of scarcity, to cele-brate, know, help, and—dangerous as the word seems to us today—love one another. But nothing in my survey of the early school years offers children such a vision of education, on which as mature adults they can draw, to live their lives in community.

The school that took seriously the goals of community skills as well as academic excellence might look something like this.

1. It would be neighborhood-based until sixth grade, making the education of children again an experience of a particular place, its streets, its greenspace, and most important, its resi-dents, history, and lore. The neighborhood school would return to the adults in the neighborhood a greater and more organic role in school life, as parents, mentors, patrons, and volunteers.

2. The school would be conceived and treated as a community in itself. Children would spend several hours a week in a

"town" meeting, a practicum facilitated by a trained professional, in which matters of community life are taken up. They
would learn about the dynamics of leadership and participation.
They would learn conflict resolution, peer review, and how to
cope with negative emotions and behavior.

This "class" would also be the incubator for a variety of projects inside and outside the school building, in which the different talents of the group would be brought into play and
affirmed in the service of the larger community (see below).

3. Each term, children would identify and complete a community project that required at least one day a week of "school"
time. For young children, this project could be as simple as
maintaining a small garden near the school building or visiting
a neighborhood nursing home. For older students, it would
involve cooperation with students from other local schools as
well as alternative and private schools in the community, businesses, and government.

4. Part of the goal in performing these projects would be for
the children to get to know and work with peers in contiguous
neighborhoods. They would also learn to ask in every instance,
"What will be the consequence of this project on the community as a whole?"

5. The school curriculum would be constructed in part around
children's listening to the stories of others in the community.
We need the stories of those we live among to know and respect the reality in which we are grounded. Listening well is
one of the basic arts of community life; it is also the way chil-

dren learn to identify teachers outside the classroom. Children should routinely hear from the elderly, local business people, librarians, new immigrants, and neighborhood officials.

6. Music would be a mandated discipline for every student in the school. Amid the welter of conflicting ideologies that have hamstrung us in education in recent years, music stands alone in having retained its objective standards of mastery. It is accessible to every language and ethnic group. It requires of each practitioner the same skills: focus, self-control, and concentration. Finally, music creates a distinctly public and communal form of beauty. It is most itself when it is shared.

7. In traditional academic subjects, greater emphasis would be placed on the relational dimension of truth. Children would learn that knowledge is reciprocal and communal. As we go about naming, categorizing, and "mastering" our environment, we are also being named and mastered, if we can learn to attend to the nonverbal, unsystematic messages coming to us from every aspect of our natural and human habitat.

What we learn is not simply for our own benefit; it is constantly implicating our conduct in community and, by the choices we make about that conduct, echoing back again to us. If we are wise, we continue to learn from the process. Formal education ought to reinforce in children the wisdom they already possess about our deep interconnection and interdependence.

8. Children would learn how to be silent for a period of time each day. They would learn to work alone, and to meditate.

Silence and solitude are the conditions in which we come into possession of our uniqueness and our capacity for intentional action. It is never too early to learn to know oneself.

9. Children would learn a traditional handcraft or skill from elderly mentors in the community, or grandparents, and teach younger siblings and neighborhood children as they grew adept.

10. The adults in the school and neighborhood would collectively and continually be engaged in asking the question: how much are we able to pass on that is of high and genuine quality? How do we balance the ever expanding universe of information with the language of memory, wisdom, and tradition?

We are mistaken if we think that by emphasizing cognitive knowledge and cutting-edge material we are only affecting children's stock of information. Knowledge must "complete itself" in community or it will be of limited value in helping them become full human beings.

Good learning is a spiritual process; the aim is wholeness, of both the individual and society. Raised to honor the profusions of information, we must re-school ourselves in a countersensibility that is deeper and older than this. Knowledge that takes its life from the community and returns to it teaches us the abiding truths: responsibility, reciprocity, the sublimation of self in the work of the collective endeavor, civilization.

Even if schools don't provide all the answers to our common and vexing questions, they ought to protect the terms of learning, which are always terms of relatedness and connection. I still don't have an adequate reply to Tracy's tears. For now, our classroom is still the street, with its squirrels and bluejays, its regular "brown truck" man and the neighbors: community, from a child's-eye view. It is the wholeness from which he will depart for larger, more disparate realms, the seamless days before the many broken sequences entailed in being a human being in our times. It will take the wisdom of a lifetime to guide him back to a place of such connections. I hope that his schooling will help him chart his way.

END NOTE: A PIECE

The way to study people is not from the top down or the bottom up, but from the inside out, from the place where people are articulate to the place where they are not.

—HENRY GLASSIE, *Passing the Time in Ballymenone*, 1982

MY SON AND I have a nightly ritual. Just as he is ready to drop off to sleep, the usual array of favorite tales having been read, I weave one last story out of the day's events, told through the characters of two barnyard creatures. Their antics try to teach him something about himself, or help resolve some childhood dilemma, before the day is done. And every night when I am finished and have exhausted every narrative gambit in my bag of tricks (and am nearly asleep myself in his bedroom rocker), his small whisper comes.

"One more piece, Mommy."

This piece is a form entirely of his creation. It shares little with a story except a mother's voice. A fragment, it is mainly an attempt to stave off closure, without necessary connection to anything that has gone before. Yet it satisfies. It satisfies his sense of pacing and presence and the awareness that behind the stories resides the larger mind of she who goes about her days filled with many preoccupations besides elves, who will show up for breakfast and maintain the mysterious structures of the home.

So here is a piece, just before the silence. Words given over to sleep and, perhaps tomorrow, to acts. In the work of making home, this is always a good point to remember—that words are one thing, acts another—since life is always waiting, ever larger and more complicated than our stories about it.

The house is quiet as I write. The few cars outside pass in a dreamscape of fallen leaves. Just a few hours ago we celebrated our annual Lantern Festival. A thousand strong, we gather at the pond as darkness falls. Babies in strollers and grandparents, teens and a few curiosity-seekers, we observe the year's turn toward darkness and in the face of it stake our claim to the vestigial light we will cling to through a spare season.

One by one we light the candles stuck into the bottoms of old Coke bottles that we've covered with bits of pasted tissue paper. Then we fan out, mapping the darkness with tiny lights. We draw a meandering strand along the wooded path, and as we move, we sing. Bits of lullabies, spirituals, old movement songs. Here and there patches of reflected light begin to pierce the surface of the pond like bits of stained glass. A low pulse of wonder starts to take hold as, one by one, bound by nothing more than the desire to create something beautiful, something whole, we watch a form in the process of coming to life.

Within half an hour the first and the last of us meet, and we stop. Before us spans a ring of light—watchful, ardent, faithful—and it is ourselves. In its spell we draw a bit closer to one another, rapt at what is still possible among human beings on this rapacious, disjunct planet, the ability to create a shared experience of meaning. Others might call it local culture. We experience it simply as belonging.

Finally, just as there is no discrete beginning to this lovely, breathtaking moment, there is never any particular point at which it could accurately be said to end. We simply turn and break away. Coddling the flames in our lanterns, we make our way back through the streets and to our homes. But the singing doesn't end. From the hills and the low roads, the spell trails us. At front doors up and down the streets of the neighborhood, we blow out our candles and enter our houses. We hang our lanterns in the kitchen, where they will remain well through Thanksgiving, until holiday greens relegate them to closet or cellar.

I have done little to make this evening special except to turn up with my unlit candle. Eight years ago it was much the same story. I moved in with uncertain lights of my own, looking for a steady flame. Less for brilliance than for warmth; not so much to be seen as to be illuminated. And over time I've come to know that this warmth is essential.

Warmth has always played such a role. Think about the small bands of pioneers, half-crazed with dream and fear on the edge of the unknown we then called the frontier. The campfire was their hope on the frigid verge—of day and every other act of becoming. It was courage when the ground underfoot refused to change, then and there, from arid rock to riverbank.

Out past my stoop is another kind of frontier. Like most city places, it is a collection of groups pronounced enough to offer their members sanctuary from the edgy frays of pluralism. My immediate neighbors, for instance, include a gay couple. An

Episcopal priest. Two spinster sisters. An unmarried Jewish woman with an adopted Peruvian child. A Puerto Rican lawyer and his Native American wife. And it would not be difficult for us to live the same fractionated lives that others do in the face of the urban frontier's uncertainty, except that we don't. I have tried to understand why. And I think that it has most to do with this thing I call warmth, a certain tenor maintained by the continual overlapping of lives that share a common devotion to place.

All of us were drawn here in search of a home in the world. My gay friends came because word got around that this was a safe place: low-key and tolerant. Art students have long known that a colony of fellow travelers had secured the marginal fringes. My high-powered surgeon friend Phil traded a spread in the exclusive suburb of Chestnut Hill for city digs and lower taxes, closer to his work. Eva, the young woman who cared for my son when he was an infant, lives here so that she can stay connected to her extended Honduran family and raise her children in her language and traditions; and Kim, because he and the other survivors of the Khmer Rouge had simply traveled far enough, for peace and a modest livelihood.

We came for the warmth, knowing others before us had gone to extraordinary lengths to protect its indigenous, authentic character. They understood that the search for home is essentially the search not for comfort but for meaning; that meaning always entails a measure of integration; and that integration requires that we learn to live well with complexity.

———————

We Americans are a people with a peculiar notion of simplicity. We imagine that life will be happier in every respect if it is simple, so we construct habitats, transport systems, dwellings that minimize unwonted complexity, problems we can't solve, and people we don't understand. We imagine—particularly in an age of massive image bombardment, info fragments, and aural junk—that such simplicity will keep us focused, keep us strong.

The suburbs, of course, were the first thrust toward this unencumberedness in postwar times, the cars, strip malls, and tract housing devices Americans used to pursue their private quest for the good life in relative—well—privacy. But the city quickly caught up, and, if anything, today surpasses this earlier exemplar. Subways and border freeways move us from work to recreation to culture—to worship, even. Neighborhoods have become fortified encampments, guarded zones of noncomplexity, to which residents return at night to neighbors much like themselves, after days spent with little or no meaningful interaction with anyone who is not. This is as true for the poor as for the rich, the only difference being that if you are poor you subside in a much less traveled zone, the hopeless zone. It is no wonder we've grown so fascinated by the ultimate images of retreat and focused serenity, of homesteading in Montana, cloisters and monasteries. But only a fool would argue that this selective association and segmentation, this distorted "simplicity," has made us strong, psychologically, socially, or culturally.

Jamaica Plain is different. It is the strongest, most empowered community I've ever known, and it has taught me to cherish a radically different way of life. We talk to one another here.

We try, some to a greater degree than others, to embrace one another's burdens. We actually do delight in each other, rejoice together, mourn together, labor together, as John Winthrop exhorted his early band of Puritans to do in their new land.

Why do we do it? I can only tell you with absolute certainty *how* we do it. And I can tell you with equal conviction that you'll never find a book or an expert who can answer, definitively and rationally, once and for all, why a place like ours functions as a community, because it is not an achievement of the educated mind but of the simple heart.

One thing seems clear. To the extent that we see our "place" as an integral element in our personal well-being, one of the necessary dimensions of an integrated self, a whole range of previously meaningless information starts to matter a great deal. We begin to engage in many new dialogues, for a place, unlike a career or wealth or even simplicity, is inevitably shared. Place is the most public and fundamental source of community that we have. When we care about our place, we find ourselves talking about local speed bumps, or how to maintain our kids' friendships when they are in many different schools. We talk about a new real estate development a block away, about preserving a historic landmark near the pond. The lives around us start to matter more. They don't supplant those relationships we've brought along with us and that continue to claim our identification with worlds beyond our neighborhoods. But they begin to figure more than we might have expected. We scan the weekly paper looking for names we know, places or institutions whose fate has become part of our own. In the process, community becomes less proscriptive than fluid. It becomes the warmth that upholds and shapes us. And one day we wake up and find that our lives have become surprisingly complex, and unexpectedly meaningful.

I look up and watch the maple leaves, always the first to fling themselves earthward, and consider again this thing we have called simplicity. Our most enduring collective fantasy is that our progenitors in a raw land fought tooth and nail for unencumbrance and personal freedom. We've told ourselves, until we are sick with the repetition, that this has always been, and will be, our way, and that our legal, economic, social, and even family institutions must follow suit.

Our error, it seems to me from my small porch looking out into darkness, is that we've pitted personal freedom against community and conflated simplicity with disengagement. We forget that the few whose coming had *any* philosophical underpinning, aside from advantage or survival, came to protect a set of values and a communal way of life. Their lot was cast together; together they prevailed against oppression.

Past my stoop is another kind of frontier, and beyond it all manner of oppression: the tyranny of isolation and loneliness, the collapse of collective values, the disintegration of local economies at the hands of distant money managers, the oppression of despair and massive waste.

We have rediscovered here the only power that matters in countering oppression, individually and collectively, and it is a meaningful complexity, the day-in-and-day-out effort to balance our individual pursuits with what is of value to us collectively. It is the challenge of casting and keeping our flames. In complex communities, we are met and affirmed, challenged, broadened, and held accountable. Here we need to maneuver and strain, travel and spend, far less than our counterparts elsewhere to meet up with our humanity. And having to search no further than our neighbors for a sense of meaning, we are free to work the earth more deeply where we are.

The Shakers, one of the earlier successor offshoots of the Puritans, settled in the valleys of central Massachusetts not far from here. Probably their greatest legacy, aside from their interpretive simplicity of style, is the enduring folk tune that captures the element of the gift in all of this: "'Tis a gift to be simple, 'tis a gift to be free." The Shakers knew that true simplicity is a complex and never-ending task, and the "coming down right" impossible to achieve without a community in which we can encounter all the bendings and bowings of the self that give us any chance of becoming mature persons and true citizens.

Most of us here didn't come to Jamaica Plain to change the world, and we have done only the little bit we can to contribute to its special ways. What happens here is a quiet sort of convergence, between the living by one's own lights and the bearing of them out into the public paths. It is how life is meant to be lived. One Sunday evening, we hang the lantern at the window and slide into bed knowing that, come daybreak, it will still be warm.

ACKNOWLEDGMENTS

The themes I have taken up in this book were conceived during my fifteen years as a journalist of urban affairs. They would have remained untried precepts had it not been for the residents of my community. Their vision, passion, and commitment—their sheer aliveness—roused me to attempt to see the common life whole and to share some of its lessons.

There are others, to whom my debt is incalculable:

Alan Lupo, first gentleman of the tales of this and other local places;

Sam Lloyd, rector of Trinity Church, who shone a good light through the dark passes;

Lynn Runnells, painter and sage, who led me to stones and sat with me while I read them; and

the poet Anne Carson, for her friendship and encouragement.

My editor, Elisabeth Kallick Dyssegaard, saw before there were images, and believed.

I could have done nothing without Jane Lynch, and later the teachers at the Apple Orchard, who ensured my son's happiness and health while I wrote; Pam Hatchfield, Mitchell Tunick, and H. Perry, who made weekly feasts of our dinnertimes; nor certainly without the loving tactical assistance of the man who shares my love of ideas and discourse and *pousse rapiers*, Mark Morrow.

Several books read during the writing of this book have confirmed and deepened my understanding of community. They are: Daniel Kemmis, *Community and the Politics of Place* (Norman: University of Oklahoma Press, 1990). John McKnight, *The Careless Society: Community and Its Counterfeits* (New York: Basic Books/Harper Collins, 1995). Henry Glassie, *Passing the Time in Ballymenone* (Philadelphia: University of Pennsylvania Press, 1982). Alan Lupo, Frank Colcor, and Edmund P. Fowler, *Rites of Way: The Politics of Transportation in Boston and the U.S. City* (Boston: Little, Brown & Co., 1971). Alexander von Hoffman, *Local Attachments* (Baltimore: Johns Hopkins University Press, 1994).

Four Jamaica Plain figures whose names appear nowhere in the body of the book but whose lives are nevertheless a continuing source of inspiration to me and many others who make this home deserve mention: the artist Helen Hummel; the founder of Greater Boston Legal Services, Gary Bellow; Stavros Frantzis's partner in community-enhancing commercial development, Mordy Levin; and Christine Cooper's indispensable partner in maintaining the dynamism of the Jamaica Pond Project, Charlie Hauck.